LOVE ABOUT LOVE

ALSO BY C.K. WILLIAMS

Lies

I Am the Bitter Name

With Ignorance

Sophocles' Women of Trachis (with Gregory Dickerson)

The Lark. The Thrush. The Starling. (Poems from Issa)

Tar

Flesh and Blood

Poems 1963—1993

The Bacchae of Euripides

A Dream of Mind

Selected Poems

The Vigil

Poetry and Consciousness: Selected Essays

Repair

Misgivings: My Mother, My Father, Myself (Memoir)

LOVE ABOUT LOVE

C.K. WILLIAMS

AUSABLE PRESS

2001

The poems in this book were first published in *Lies, I Am the Bitter Name, With Ignorance, Tar, Flesh and Blood, A Dream of Mind, The Vigil,* and *Repair.* Thanks to Farrar, Straus & Giroux for permission to reprint.

Cover drawing: Jed Mauger Williams. Pastel on paper (detail), 1999.

Design and composition by Ausable Press. The type is Adobe's Jenson.
Cover design by Rebecca Soderholm.

Published by Ausable Press, 46 East Hill Road, Keene NY 12942
www.ausablepress.com

Library of Congress Control Number 00-135310
ISBN 0-9672668-2-3 (acid-free paper)
ISBN 0-9672668-3-1 (pbk.; acid-free paper).

Catherine,
for everything,

and all those others with whom I share love,
for everything else.

Contents

I. WITHIN, WITHOUT

❖ STILL LIFE

All we do—how old are we? I must be twelve, she a little older;
    thirteen, fourteen—is hold hands
and wander out behind a barn, past a rusty hay rake, a half-
    collapsed old Model T,
then down across a barbed-wire gated pasture—early emerald
    ryegrass, sumac in the dip—
to where a brook, high with run-off from a morning storm, broad-
    ened and spilled over—
turgid, muddy, viscous, snagged here and there with shattered
    branches—in a bottom meadow.

I don't know then that the place, a mile from anywhere, and day,
    brilliant, sultry, balmy,
are intensifying everything I feel, but I know now that what made
    simply touching her
almost a consummation was as much the light, the sullen surge of
    water through the grass,
the coils of scent, half hers—the unfamiliar perspiration, talc,
    something else I'll never place—
and half the air's: mown hay somewhere, crushed clover under-
    foot, the brook, the breeze.

I breathe it still that breeze, and, not knowing how I know for
    certain that it's that,
although it is, I know, exactly that, I drag it in and drive it—rich,
    delicious,
as biting as wet tin—down, my mind casting up flickers to fit it—
    another field, a hollow—

and now her face, even it, frail and fine, comes momentarily to
    focus, and her hand,
intricate and slim, the surprising firmness of her clasp, how judi-
    ciously it meshes mine.

All we do—how long does it last? an hour or two, not even one
    whole afternoon:
I'll never see her after that, and, strangely (strange even now), not
    mind, as though,
in that afternoon the revelations weren't only of the promises of
    flesh, but of resignation—
all we do is trail along beside the stream until it narrows, find the
    one-log bridge
and cross into the forest on the other side: silent footfalls, hills, a
    crest, a lip.

I don't know then how much someday—today—I'll need it all,
    how much want to hold it,
and, not knowing why, not knowing still how time can tempt us
    so emphatically and yet elude us,
not have it, not the way I would, not the way I want to have *that*
    day, *that* light,
the motes that would have risen from the stack of straw we leaned
    on for a moment,
the tempered warmth of air which so precisely seemed the coef-
    ficient of my fearful ardor,

not, after all, even the objective place, those shifting paths I can't
    really follow now
but only can compile from how many other ambles into other
    woods, other stoppings in a glade—

(4)

(for a while we were lost, and frightened; night was just beyond
     the hills; we circled back)—
even, too, her gaze, so darkly penetrating, then lifting idly past, is
     so much imagination,
a portion of that figured veil we cast against oblivion, then try,
     with little hope, to tear away.

❖ FOR GAIL, WHEN I WAS FIVE

My soul is out back eating your soul.
I have you tied in threads like a spider
and I am drinking down your laughter
in huge spoonfuls. It is like tinsel.
It sprays over the crusty peach baskets
and the spades hung on pegs. It is like air
and you are screaming, or I am, and we are
in different places with wild animal faces.

What does God do to children who touch
in the darkness of their bodies and laugh?
What does he think of little underpants
that drift down on the hose like flowers?
God eats your soul, like me. He drinks
your laughter. It is God in the history
of my body who melts your laughter
and spits it in the wounds of my life like tears.

❖ FIRST DESIRES

It was like listening to the record of a symphony before you knew
    anything at all about the music,
what the instruments might sound like, look like, what portion of
    the orchestra each represented:
there were only volumes and velocities, thickenings and thin-
    nings, the winding cries of change
that seemed to touch within you, through your body, to be part of
    you and then apart from you.
And even when you'd learned the grainy timbre of the single
    violin, the ardent arpeggios of the horn,
when you tried again there were still uneases and confusions left,
    an ache, a sense of longing
that held you in chromatic dissonance, droning on beyond the
    dominant's resolve into the tonic,
as though there were a flaw of logic in the structure, or in (you
    knew it was more likely) you.

❖ IN THERE

Here I am, walking along your eyelid again
toward your tear duct. Here are your eyelashes
like elephant grass and one tear
blocking the way like a boulder.

It probably takes me a long time
to figure it out, chatting with neighbors,
trying penicillin, steam baths, meditation
on the Shekinah and sonnet cycles

and then six more months blasting
with my jackhammer before I get in there
and can wander through your face, meeting you
on the sly, kissing you from this side.

I am your own personal verb now. Here I come,
"dancing," "loving," "making cookies."
I find a telescope
and an old astronomer

to study my own face with,
and then, well, I am dreaming behind your cheekbone
about Bolivia and tangerines and the country
and here I come again, along your eyelid, walking.

❖ THE ORCHID

with thanks to Curtis Ingham

"Tell me to touch your breast," I wanted to say: "Please, please,
   please touch my breast,"
I thought she wanted to say, but was too frightened, like me, too
   overwhelmed, too stricken,
like me, with the surges and furies of need; our lips, locked,
   ground together again and again,
we were bruised and swollen, like lovers in stories, sweating like
   lovers in bed, but no bed.
Then I heard, I thought, "Touch me," and ecstatic, I touched, but
   she brushed me away like a fly…
No, still held me, only my hand fell like a fly, her thirsty lips drank
   from me what they needed.
My testicles trembled, the orchid I'd paid five dollars for, hooked
   to the wires of her bra,
browned, faded, crumpled between us, as the orchid of memory
   crumples, mummified like a fly.

❖ TO MARKET

suppose I move a factory
in here in my head in my
breast in my left hand I'm moving
dark machines in with gear boxes
and floaters and steel cams
that turn over and start things
I'm moving in fibers through
my left nostril and trucks
under my nipples and the union
has its bathroom where I think
and the stockbroker his desk
where I love

and then if I started turning
out goods and opening
shops with glass counters and rugs
what if I said
to you this is how men live and I
want to would you believe me
and love me I have my little
lunch box and my thermos and
I walk along like one leg
on the way to work swearing
I love you and we have lunch
behind the boiler and I promise
I love you and meanwhile the oil
flowing switches steam wrenches
metal I love

you and things finish get shined
up packed in streamers
mailed and I love you
meanwhile all this while I love
you and I'm being bought pieces
of me at five dollars
and parts at ten cents and
here I am still saying I love
you under the stacks under
the windows with wires the smoke
going up I love
you I love you

❖ EVEN IF I COULD

Except for the little girl
making faces behind me, and the rainbow
behind her, and the school and the truck,
the only thing between you
and infinity
is me. Which is why you cover your ears
when I speak and why
you're always oozing around the edges,
clinging, trying
to go by me.

And except for my eyes and the back
of my skull, and then my hair,
the wall, the concrete
and the fire-cloud, except for them
you would see
God. And that's why rage howls in your arms
like a baby and why I can't move—
because of the thunder and the shadows
merging like oil and the smile gleaming
through the petals.

Let me tell you how sick with loneliness
I am. What can I do while the distance
throbs on my back like a hump,
or say, with stars stinging me
through the wheel? You are before me,
behind me things rattle their deaths out

like paper. The angels ride
in their soft saddles:
except for them, I would come closer
and go.

❖ SAINT SEX

there are people whose sex
keeps growing even when they're old whose
genitals swell like tumors endlessly
until they are all sex and nothing else nothing
that moves or thinks nothing
but great inward and outward handfuls of gristle

think of them men
who ooze their penises out like snail
feet whose testicles clang in their scrotums women
are like anvils to them the world an
anvil they want to take whole buildings
in their arms they want
to come in the windows to run antennas
through their ducts like ramrods and women
these poor women who dream and dream of
the flower they can't sniff it sends buds
into their brain they feel their neural
river clot with moist fingers the ganglia
hardening like ant eggs the ends
burning off

pity them these people there are no wars
for them there is no news no
summer no reason they are so humble they want
nothing they have no hands or faces
pity them at night whispering I love
you to themselves and during the day how they

walk along smiling and suffering pity
them love them they are
angels

❖ ON THE ROOF

The trouble with me is that whether I get love or not
I suffer from it. My heart always seems to be prowling
a mile ahead of me, and, by the time I get there to surround it,
it's chewing fences in the next county, clawing
the bank-vault wall down or smashing in the window
I'd just started etching my name on with my diamond.

And that's how come I end up on the roof. Because even if I talk
into my fist everyone still hears my voice like the ocean
in theirs, and so they solace me and I have to keep
breaking toes with my gun-boots and coming up here
to live—by myself, like an aerial, with a hand on the ledge,
one eye glued to the tin door and one to the skylight.

❖ YOURS

I'd like every girl in the world to have a poem of her own
I've written for her I don't even want to make love to them all
      anymore
just write things your body makes me delirious your face enchants
      me
you are a wonder of soul spirit intelligence one for every one
and then the men I don't care whether I can still beat them all
them too a poem for them how many?
seeing you go through woods like part of the woods seeing you
      play piano
seeing you hold your child in your tender devastating hands
and of course the children too little poems they could sing or
      dance to
this is our jumping game this our seeing game our holding each
      other
even the presidents with all their death the congressmen and
      judges
I'd give them something
they would hold awed to their chests as their proudest life thing
somebody walking along a road where there's no city would look
      up
and see his poem coming down like a feather out of nowhere
or on the assembly line new instructions a voice sweet as
      lunch-time
or she would turn over a stone by the fire and if she couldn't read
it would sing to her in her body
listen! everyone! you have your own poem now
it's yours as much as your heart as much as your own life is

you can do things to it shine it up iron it dress it in doll clothes
o men! o people! please stop how it's happening now please
I'm working as fast as I can I can't stop to use periods
sometimes I draw straight lines on the page because the words .
are too slow
I can only do one at a time don't die first please
don't give up and start crying or hating each other they're coming
I'm hurrying be patient there's still time isn't there? isn't there?

❖ THE GAS STATION

This is before I'd reach Nietzsche. Before Kant or Kierkegaard,
    even before Whitman and Yeats.
I don't think there were three words in my head yet. I knew,
    perhaps, that I should suffer,
I can remember I almost cried for this or for that, nothing special,
    nothing to speak of.
Probably I was mad with grief for the loss of my childhood, but I
    wouldn't have known that.
It's dawn. A gas station. Route twenty-two. I remember exactly:
    route twenty-two curved,
there was a squat, striped concrete divider they'd put in after a
    plague of collisions.
The gas station? Texaco, Esso—I don't know. They were just
    words anyway then, just what their signs said.
I wouldn't have understood the first thing about monopoly or
    imperialist or oppression.
It's dawn. It's so late. Even then, when I was never tired, I'm just
    holding on.
Slumped on my friend's shoulder, I watch the relentless, wordless
    misery of the route twenty-two sky
that seems to be filming my face with a grainy oil I keep trying to
    rub off or in.
Why are we here? Because one of my friends, in the men's room
    over there, has blue balls.
He has to jerk off. I don't know what that means, "blue balls," or
    why he has to do that—
it must be important to have to stop here after this long night, but
    I don't ask.

I'm just trying, I think, to keep my head as empty as I can for as
    long as I can.
One of my other friends is asleep. He's so ugly, his mouth
    hanging, slack and wet.
Another—I'll never see this one again—stares from the window
    as though he were frightened.
Here's what we've done. We were in Times Square, a pimp found
    us, corralled us, led us somewhere,
down a dark street, another dark street, up dark stairs, dark hall,
    dark apartment,
where his whore, his girl or his wife or his mother for all I know
    dragged herself from her sleep,
propped herself on an elbow, gazed into the dark hall, and agreed,
    for two dollars each, to take care of us.
Take care of us. Some of the words that come through me now
    seem to stay, to hook in.
My friend in the bathroom is taking so long. The filthy sky must
    be starting to lighten.
It took me a long time, too, with the woman, I mean. Did I
    mention that she, the woman, the whore or mother,
was having her time and all she would deign do was to blow us?
    Did I say that? Deign? Blow?
What a joy, though, the idea was in those days. Blown! What a
    thing to tell the next day.
She only deigned, though, no more. She was like a machine.
    When I lift her back to me now,
there's nothing there but that dark, curly head, working, a ma-
    chine, up and down, and now,
Freud, Marx, Fathers, tell me, what am I, doing this, telling this,
    on her, on myself,

hammering it down, cementing it, sealing it in, but a machine, too?
  Why am I doing this?
I still haven't read Augustine. I don't understand Chomsky that
  well. Should I?
My friend at last comes back. Maybe the right words were there
  all along. *Complicity. Wonder.*
How pure we were then, before Rimbaud, before Blake. *Grace.
  Love. Take care of us. Please.*

❖ GIRL MEETS BOY

She would speak of "our relationship" as though it were a thing
    apart from either of us,
an entity with separate necessities, even its own criteria for ap-
    praisal, judgment, mode of act,
to which both of us were to be ready to sacrifice our own more
    momentary notions of identity.
It was as though there were a pre-existent formula or recipe,
    something from a textbook,
which demanded not only the right ingredients—attentiveness,
    affection, generosity, et cetera—
but also a constant and rigorous examination and analysis of the
    shifting configurations
our emotions were assuming in their presumed movement
    toward some ultimate consummation
in whose intensity the rest of this, not an end, would be re-
    deemed, to wither quietly away.

❖ FAT

The young girl jogging in mittens and skimpy gym shorts through
    a freezing rainstorm up our block
would have a perfect centerfold body except for the bulbs of
    grandmotherly fat on her thighs.
Who was it again I loved once. . . no, not loved truly, liked,
    somewhat, and slept with, a lot,
who when she'd brood on the I thought quite adorable blubber
    she had there would beat it on the wall?
Really: she'd post herself naked half a stride back, crouch like a
    skier, and swing her hips, bang!
onto the plaster, bang! ten times, a hundred: bang! the wall shook,
    bang! her poor body quivered.
I'd lie there aghast, I knew that mad pounding had to mean more
    than itself, of course I thought me.
For once I was right; soon after, she left me, and guess what, for all
    that, I missed her.

❖ GARDENS

The ever-consoling fantasy of my early adolescence was that one
      day time would stop for me:
everything in the world, for however long I wanted it to, would
      stay frozen in a single instant,
the clock on the classroom wall, the boring teacher, the other kids
      . . . all but someone else and me,
Arlene and me, Marie and me, Barbara of the budding breasts,
      Sheila of the braids and warming smile . . .
In the nurse's room was a narrow cot, there we would repair, there
      we would reveal ourselves.
One finds of course to one's amazement and real chagrin that such
      things actually happen,
the precocious male, the soon to be knocked-up girl, but by now
      that's no longer what we care about:
what matters now are qualities of longing, this figment, fragment,
      its precious, adorable irresolutions.

◆ FIFTEEN

for Jessie

You give no hint how shy you really are, so thoroughly your warm
      and welcoming temperament masks
those confounding and to me still painful storms of adolescent ill
      at ease, confusion and disruption.
Our old father-daughter stroll down South Street these days is
      like a foray into the territories—
the weighings and the longings, young men, men of age, the
      brazen or sidelong subliminal proposings:
you're fair game now, but if you notice, you manage to keep it
      unimpeachably to yourself,
your newly braceless smile good-humoredly desexualizing the
      leering and licentious out-there.
Innocently you sheathe yourself in the most patently innocuous
      and unpremeditated innocence;
even with me, though, your kiss goodbye is layered: cheek toward,
      body swayed imperceptibly away.

❖ SIXTEEN: TUSCANY

Wherever Jessie and her friend Maura alight, clouds of young
    men suddenly appear like bees.
We're to meet in Florence at the Ponte Vecchio at nine o'clock:
    they're twenty minutes early,
two vacationing Sicilian bees, hair agleam like fenders, are begging
    for a kiss good night when we arrive.
At San Gimignano, on the steps that go down from the church
    into the square—such clean breezes—
two Tuscan bees, lighter, handsome: great flurried conferences
    with references to pocket dictionary
to try to find out where we're staying, how long staying, how get
    there . . .impossible, poor bees.
A broad blond bee from Berkeley at the bank in Lucca; in Pisa,
    French bees, German bees . . .
The air is filled with promises of pollen, the dancing air is filled
    with honeyed wings and light.

❖ THE DOG

Except for the dog, that she wouldn't have him put away, wouldn't
    let him die, I'd have liked her.
She was handsome, busty, chunky, early middle-aged, very black,
    with a stiff, exotic dignity
that flurried up in me a mix of warmth and sexual apprehension
    neither of which, to tell the truth,
I tried very hard to nail down: she was that much older and in
    those days there was still the race thing.
This was just at the time of civil rights: the neighborhood I was
    living in was mixed.
In the narrow streets, the tiny three-floored houses they called
    father-son-holy-ghosts
which had been servants' quarters first, workers' tenements, then
    slums, still were, but enclaves of us,
beatniks and young artists, squatted there and commerce be-
    tween everyone was fairly easy.
Her dog, a grinning mongrel, rib and knob, gristle and grizzle,
    wasn't terribly offensive.
The trouble was that he was ill, or the trouble more exactly was
    that I had to know about it.
She used to walk him on a lot I overlooked, he must have had a
    tumor or a blockage of some sort
because every time he moved his bowels, he shrieked, a chilling,
    almost human scream of anguish.
It nearly always caught me unawares, but even when I'd see them
    first, it wasn't better.
The limp leash coiled in her hand, the woman would be profiled
    to the dog, staring into the distance,

apparently oblivious, those breasts of hers like stone, while he, not
    a step away, laboring,

trying to eject the feeble, mucus-coated, blood-flecked chains that
    finally spurted from him,

would set himself on tiptoe and hump into a question mark, one
    quivering back leg grotesquely lifted.

Every moment he'd turn his head, as though he wanted her, to no
    avail, to look at him,

then his eyes would dim and he'd drive his wounded anus in the
    dirt, keening uncontrollably,

lurching forward in a hideous, electric dance as though someone
    were at him with a club.

When at last he'd finish, she'd wipe him with a tissue like a child;
    he'd lick her hand.

It was horrifying; I was always going to call the police; once I
    actually went out to chastise her—

didn't she know how selfish she was, how the animal was
    suffering?—she scared me off, though.

She was older than I'd thought, for one thing, her flesh was
    loosening, pouches of fat beneath the eyes,

and poorer, too, shabby, tarnished: I imagined smelling some-
    thing faintly acrid as I passed.

Had I ever really mooned for such a creature? I slunk around the
    block, chagrined, abashed.

I don't recall them too long after that. Maybe the dog died, maybe
    I was just less sensitive.

Maybe one year when the cold came and I closed my windows, I
    forgot them . . . then I moved.

Everything was complicated now, so many tensions, so much
    bothersome self-consciousness.

Anyway, those back streets, especially in bad weather when the
    ginkgos lost their leaves, were bleak.
It's restored there now, ivy, pointed brick, garden walls with
    broken bottles mortared on them,
but you'd get sick and tired then: the rubbish in the gutter, the
    general sense of dereliction.
Also, I'd found a girl to be in love with: all we wanted was to live
    together, so we did.

❖ LOVE

Youth

Except for the undeniable flash of envy I feel, the reflexive
    competitiveness, he's inconsequential:
all I even see of him is the nape of his neck with his girlfriend's
    fingers locked in his hair.
She, though, looks disturbingly like a girl I wanted and pestered
    and who I thought broke my heart
when I was at that age of being all absorbed in just the unattain-
    abilities she represented.
With what unashamed ardor this one is kissing, head working,
    that hand tugging him ever tighter,
and when at last they come apart, with what *gratitude* she peers at
    him, staring into his eyes
with what looks like nothing but relief, as though she'd waited her
    whole life for this, died for this,
time has taken so long for this, I thought you'd never get here, I
    thought I'd wither first and fade.

Beginnings

They're at that stage where so much desire streams between
    them, so much frank need and want,
so much absorption in the other and the self and the self-admiring
    entity and unity they make—
her mouth so full, breast so lifted, head thrown back *so* far in her
    laughter at his laughter,

he so solid, planted, oaky, firm, so resonantly factual in the head-
iness of being craved so,
she almost wreathed upon him as they intertwine again, touch
again, cheek, lip, shoulder, brow,
every glance moving toward the sexual, every glance away soaring
back in flame into the sexual—
that just to watch them is to feel again that hitching in the groin,
that filling of the heart,
the old, sore heart, the battered, foundered, faithful heart, snort-
ing again, stamping in its stall.

Habit

He has his lips pressed solidly against her cheek, his eyes are wide
open, though, and she, too,
gazes into the distance, or at least is nowhere in the fragile com-
position they otherwise create.
He breaks off now, sulkily slouches back; his hand, still lifted to
her face, idly cups her chin,
his fingers casually drumming rhythms on her lips, a gesture she
finds not at all remarkable—
she still gazes away, looking for whatever she's been looking for,
her inattention like a wall.
Now he kisses her *again*, and they both, like athletes, hold that
way again, perversely persevering . . .
Oh, Paolo, oh, Francesca: is this all it comes to, the perturbations
and the clamor, the broken breath,
the careenings on the wheel: just this: the sorrowing flame of
consciousness so miserably dimmed?

Loss

He's the half-respectable wino who keeps to himself, camping
    with his bags on the steps of the *Bourse.*
She's the neighborhood schizo, our nomad, our pretty post-teen
    princess gone to the grim gutter:
her appalling matted hair, vile hanging rags, the engrossing
    shadow plays she acts out to herself.
Tonight, though, something takes her, she stops, waits, and
    smiling cunningly asks him for a smoke.
They both seem astonished, both their solitudes emerge, stiff-
    legged, blinking, from their lairs.
The air is charged with timid probings, promises, wants and lost
    wants, but suddenly she turns,
she can't do it, she goes, and he, with a stagy, blasé worldwear-
    iness leans back and watches,
like Orpheus watches as she raptly picks her way back to the silver
    path, back to the boiling whispers.

Sight

When she's not looking in his eyes, she looks down at his lips, his
    chin, collar, tie, back again.
When he's not looking in her eyes—her cheek, parted mouth,
    neck, breasts, thighs, back again.
Sometimes their four hands will lock and in a smooth contortion
    end up at her waist, then his waist,
then up between them, weaving, writhing, with so much anima-
    tion that their glances catch there.
The first time he looks away, she still smiles at him, smugly, with
    a lusciousness almost obscene,

then her gaze goes trailing after, as if afraid to be abandoned, as if
    desiring even what he sees.

The second time, it might be with some small suspicion that her
    eyes go quickly chasing his;

the third, they're hardening, triangulating, calculating, like a com-
    bat sergeant's on the line.

Petulance

She keeps taking poses as they eat so that her cool glance goes off
    at perpendiculars to him.

She seems to think she's hiding what she feels, that she looks
    merely interested, sophisticated.

Sometimes she leans her head on her hand, sometimes with a
    single finger covers her lower lip.

He, too, will prop his temple on his fist, as though to make her
    believe he's lost in thought.

Otherwise he simply chews, although the muscles of his jaws rise
    violently in iron ridges.

Their gazes, when they have to go that way, pass blankly over one
    another like offshore lights.

So young they are for this, to have arrived at this, both are
    suffering so and neither understands,

although to understand wouldn't mean to find relief or overcome,
    that this, too, is part of it.

Intimacy

They were so exceptionally well got-up for an ordinary Sunday
    afternoon stop-in at Deux Magots,

she in very chic deep black, he in a business suit, and they were so
      evidently just out of bed
but with very little to say to one another, much gazing off, ela-
      borate lightings of her cigarettes,
she more proper than was to be believed, sipping with a flourished
      pinky at her Pimm's Cup,
that it occurred to me I was finally seeing one of those intriguing
      Herald Tribune classifieds—
a woman's name, a number—for "escorts" or "companions," but
      then I had to change my mind:
she'd leaned toward him, deftly lifted a line of his thinning hair,
      and idly, with a mild pat,
had laid it back—not commiserating, really, just keeping record
      of the progress of the loss.

Shyness

By tucking her chin in toward her chest, she can look up darkly
      through her lashes at him,
that look of almost anguished vulnerability and sensitivity, a soft,
      near-cry of help,
the implication of a deeply privileged and sole accessibility . . .
      yours alone, yours, yours alone,
but he's so flagrantly uncertain of himself, so clearly frightened,
      that he edges into comedy:
though everybody at the party is aware she's seducing him, he
      doesn't seem to understand;
he diddles with his silly mustache, grins and gawks, gabbles away
      around her about this and that.
Now she's losing interest, you can see it; she starts to glance away,
      can't he see it? Fool!

Touch her! Reach across, just caress her with a finger on her
cheek: fool, fool—only touch her!

Wrath

He was very much the less attractive of the two: heavyset, part
punk, part L. L. Bean,
both done ineptly; his look as brutal as the bully's who tormented
you in second grade.
She was delicate and pretty; what she was suffering may have
drawn her features finer.
As I went by, he'd just crossed his arms and said, "*You're* the one
who's fucking us all up!"
He snarled it with a cruelty which made him look all the more a
thug, and which astonished me,
that he would dare to speak to her like that, be so unafraid of
losing her unlikely beauty . . .
But still, I knew, love, what he was feeling: the hungering for
reason, for fair play,
the lust for justice; all the higher systems "Go": the need, the fear,
the awe, burned away.

The Dance

They're not quite overdressed, just a bit attentively, flashily for
seventy-five or eighty.
Both wear frosted, frozen, expensive but still delicately balanced
and adhering wigs,
and both have heavy makeup: his could pass for a Miami winter
tan, but hers goes off the edge—

ice-pink lipstick, badly drawn, thick mascara arching like a balle-
rina's toward the brow.
All things considered, she's not built that badly; he has his gut
sucked nearly neatly in;
their dancing is flamboyant, well rehearsed, old-time ballroom
swirls, deft romantic dips and bows.
If only they wouldn't contrive to catch our eyes so often, to
acknowledge with ingratiating grins:
the waltz of life, the waltz of death, and still the heart-work left
undone, the heavy heart, left undone.

❖ FLOOR

A dirty picture, a photograph, possibly a tintype, from the turn of
the century, even before:
the woman is obese, gigantic; a broad, black corset cuts from un-
der her breasts to the top of her hips,
her hair is crimped, wiry, fastened demurely back with a bow one
incongruous wing of which shows.
Her eyebrows are straight and heavy, emphasizing her frank,
unintrospective plainness
and she looks directly, easily into the camera, her expression
somewhere between play and scorn,
as though the activities of the photographer were ridiculous or
beneath her contempt, or,
rather, as though the unfamiliar camera were actually the much
more interesting presence here
and how absurd it is that the lens be turned toward her and her
partner and not back on itself.
One sees the same look—pride, for some reason, is in it, and a
surprisingly sophisticated self-distancing—
in the snaps anthropologists took in backwaters during those
first, politically preconscious,
golden days of culture-hopping, and, as Goffman notes, in certain
advertisements, now.

The man is younger than the woman. Standing, he wears what
looks like a bathing costume,
black and white tank top, heavy trousers bunched in an ungainly
heap over his shoes, which are still on.

He has an immigrant's mustache he's a year or two too callow for,
    but, thick and dark, it will fit him.
He doesn't, like the woman, watch the camera, but stares ahead,
    not at the woman but slightly over and past,
and there's a kind of withdrawn, almost vulnerable thoughtful-
    ness or preoccupation about him
despite the gross thighs cast on his waist and the awkward, surely
    bothersome twist
his body has been forced to assume to more clearly exhibit the
    genital penetration.
He seems, in fact, abstracted—oblivious wouldn't be too strong a
    word—as though, possibly,
as unlikely as it would seem, he had been a virgin until now and
    was trying amid all this unholy confusion—
the hooded figure, the black box with its eye—trying, and from
    the looks of it even succeeding
in obliterating everything from his consciousness but the thing
    itself, the act itself,
so as, one would hope, to redeem the doubtlessly endless nights of
    the long Victorian adolescence.

The background is a painted screen: ivy, columns, clouds; some
    muse or grace or other,
heavy-buttocked, whory, flaunts her gauze and clodhops with a
    half-demented leer.
The whole thing's oddly poignant somehow, almost, like an
    antique wedding picture, comforting—
the past is sending out a tendril to us: poses, attitudes of stillness
    we've lost or given back.
Also, there's no shame in watching them, in being in the tacit
    commerce of having, like it or not,

(38)

received the business in one's hand, no titillation either, not a
    tangle, not a throb,
probably because the woman offers none of the normal symp-
    toms, even if minimal, even if contrived—
the tongue, say, wandering from the corner of the mouth, a glint
    of extra brilliance at the lash—
we associate to even the most innocuous, undramatic, parental
    sorts of passion, and the boy,
well, dragged in out of history, off Broome or South Street, all he
    is is grandpa:
he'll go back into whatever hole he's found to camp in, those
    higher-contrast tenements
with their rows of rank, forbidding beds, or not even beds, rags on
    a floor, or floor.
On the way there, there'll be policemen breaking strikers' heads,
    or micks', or sheenies',
there'll be war somewhere, in the sweatshops girls will turn to
    stone over their Singers.
Here, at least peace. Here, one might imagine, after he withdraws,
    a kind of manly focus taking him—
the glance he shoots to her is hard and sure—and, to her, a
    tenderness might come,
she might reach a hand—Sweet Prince—to touch his cheek, or
    might—who can understand these things?—
avert her face and pull him to her for a time before she squats to
    flush him out.

II. SORROW

❖ INSIGHT

1.

All under the supposition that he's helping her because she's so
     often melancholy lately,
he's pointing out certain problems with her character, but he's so
     serious, so vehement,
she realizes he's *attacking* her, to hurt, not help; she doesn't know
     what might be driving him,
but she finds she's thinking through his life for him, the losses, the
     long-forgotten sadnesses,
and though she can't come up with anything to correlate with how
     hatefully he's acting,
she thinks *something* has to be there, so she listens, nods, some-
     times she actually agrees.

2.

They're only arguing, but all at once she feels anxiety, and realizes
     she's afraid of him,
then, wondering whether she should risk expressing it to him, she
     understands she can't,
that the way he is these days he'll turn it back on her, and so she
     keeps it to herself,
then, despite herself, she wonders what their life's become to have
     to hide so much,
then comes a wave of disappointment, with herself, not him, and
     not for that initial fear,
but for some cowardice, some deeper dread that makes her ask,
     why not him?

3.

He's very distant, but when she asks him what it is, he insists it's
    nothing, though it's not,
she knows it's not, because he never seems to face her and his eyes
    won't hold on hers;
it makes her feel uncertain, clumsy, then as though she's somehow
    supplicating him:
though she wants nothing more from him than she already has—
    what would he think she'd want?—
when she tries to trust him, to believe his offhanded reassurance,
    she feels that she's pretending,
it's like a game, though very serious, like trying to talk yourself out
    of an imminent illness.

4.

If there are sides to take, he'll take the other side, against anything
    she says, to anyone:
at first she thinks it's just coincidence; after all, she knows she's
    sometimes wrong,
everyone is sometimes wrong, but with him now all there seem to
    be are sides, she's always wrong;
even when she doesn't know she's arguing, when she doesn't care,
    he finds her wrong,
in herself it seems she's wrong, she feels she should apologize, to
    someone, anyone, to him;
him, him, him; what is it that he wants from her: remorse, con-
    trition, should she just *die?*

5.

He's telling her in much too intricate detail about a film he's seen:
     she tries to change the subject,
he won't let her, and she finds she's questioning herself—must
     she be so critical, judgmental?—
then she's struck, from something in his tone, or absent from his
     tone, some lack of resonance,
that why he's going on about the movie is because there's nothing
     else to say to her,
or, worse, that there are things to say but not to her, they're too
     intimate to waste on her:
it's *she*, she thinks, who's being measured and found wanting, and
     what should she think now?

6.

This time her, her story, about something nearly noble she once
     did, a friend in trouble,
and she helped, but before she's hardly started he's made clear he
     thinks it's all a fantasy,
and she as quickly understands that what he really means is that
     her love, her love for him,
should reflexively surpass the way she loved, or claims she loved,
     the long-forgotten friend,
and with a shock of sorrow, she knows she can't tell him that, that
     the betrayal,
and certainly there is one, isn't his desire to wound, but her
     thinking that he shouldn't.

7.

She sits in his lap, she's feeling lonely, nothing serious, she just
      wants sympathy, company,
then she realizes that though she hasn't said a word, he's sensed
      her sadness and is irked,
feels that she's inflicting, as she always does, he seems to think, her
      misery on him,
so she tells herself not to be so needy anymore, for now, though,
      she just wants to leave,
except she can't, she knows that if he suspects he's let her down
      he'll be more irritated still,
and so she stays, feeling dumb and out of place, and heavy, heavier,
      like a load of stone.

8.

She experiences a pleasurable wave of nostalgia, not for her own
      past, but for his:
she can sense and taste the volume and the textures of the room he
      slept in as a child,
until she reminds herself she's never been there, never even seen
      the place, so, reluctantly,
she thinks reluctantly, she wonders if she might not be too close,
      too devoted to him,
whether she might actually be trying to become him, then she
      feels herself resolve, to her surprise,
to disengage from him, and such a sense of tiredness takes her that
      she almost cries.

9.

As usual these days he's angry with her, and because she wants
    him not to be she kisses him,
but perhaps because he's so surprised, she feels him feel her kiss
    came from some counter-anger,
then she starts to doubt herself, wondering if she might have
    meant it as he thinks she did,
as a traitor kiss, a Judas kiss, and if that's true, his anger, both his
    angers, would be justified:
look, though, how he looks at her, with bemusement, hardly
    hidden, he knows her so well,
he senses her perplexity, her swell of guilt and doubt: how he
    cherishes his wrath!

10.

Such matters end, there are healings, breakings-free; she tells
    herself they end, but still,
years later, when the call she'd dreaded comes, when he calls,
    asking why she hasn't called,
as though all those years it wasn't her who'd called, then stopped
    calling and began to wait,
then stopped waiting, healed, broke free, so when he innocently
    suggests they get together,
she says absolutely not, but feels uncertain—is she being spiteful?
    small?—and then she knows:
after this he'll cause her no more pain, though no matter how she
    wished it weren't, this is pain.

❖ MEDUSA

Once, in Rotterdam, a whore once, in a bar, a sailors' bar, a hooker
      bar, opened up her legs—
her legs, my god, were logs—lifted up her skirt, and rubbed
      herself, with both hands rubbed herself,
there, right there, as though what was there was something else, as
      though the something else
was something she just happened to have under there, something
      that she wanted me to see.
All I was was twenty, I was looking for a girl, the girl, the way we
      always, all of us,
looked for the girl, and the woman leaned back there and with
      both hands she mauled it,
talked to it, asked it if it wanted me, laughed and asked me if I
      wanted it, while my virginity,
that dread I'd fought so hard to lose, stone by stone was rising
      back inside me like a wall.

❖ THE NEIGHBOR

Her five horrid, deformed little dogs, who incessantly yap on the
   roof under my window;
her cats, god knows how many, who must piss on her rugs—her
   landing's a sickening reek;
her shadow, once, fumbling the chain on her door, then the door
   slamming fearfully shut:
only the barking, and the music, jazz, filtering as it does day and
   night into the hall.

The time it was Chris Conner singing "Lush Life," how it brought
   back my college sweetheart,
my first real love, who, till I left her, played the same record, and,
   head on my shoulder,
hand on my thigh, sang sweetly along, of regrets and depletions
   she was too young for,
as I was too young, later, to believe in her pain: it startled, then
   bored, then repelled me.

My starting to fancy she'd ended up in this firetrap in the Village,
   that my neighbor was her;
my thinking we'd meet, recognize one another, become friends,
   that I'd accomplish a penance;
my seeing her—it wasn't her—at the mailbox, grey-yellow hair,
   army pants under a nightgown:
her turning away, hiding her ravaged face in her hands, muttering
   an inappropriate "Hi."

Sometimes, there are frightening goings-on in the stairwell, a man
shouting *Shut up!*
the dogs frantically snarling, claws scrabbling, then her, her voice,
hoarse, harsh, hollow,
almost only a tone, incoherent, a note, a squawk, bone on metal,
metal gone molten,
calling them back, Come back, darlings; come back, dear ones, my
sweet angels, come back.

Medea she was, next time I saw her, sorceress, tranced, ecstatic,
stock-still on the sidewalk,
ragged coat hanging agape, passersby flowing around her, her
mouth torn suddenly open,
as though in a scream, silently though, as though only in her brain
or breast had it erupted:
a cry so pure, practiced, detached, it had no need of a voice or
could no longer bear one.

These invisible links that allure, these transfigurations even of
anguish that hold us:
the girl, my old love, the last, lost time I saw her, when she came
to find me at a party:
her drunkenly stumbling, falling, sprawling, skirt hiked, eyes
veined red, swollen with tears;
her shame, her dishonor; my ignorant, arrogant coarseness; my
secret pride, my turning away.

Still life on a roof top: dead trees in barrels, a bench, broken; dogs,
excrement, sky.
What pathways through pain, what junctures of vulnerability,
what crossings and counterings?

(50)

Too many lives in our lives already, too many chances for sorrow,
    too many unaccounted-for pasts.
Behold me, the god of frenzied, inexhaustible love says, rising in
    bloody splendor: *Behold me!*

Her making her way down the littered vestibule stairs, one
    agonized step at a time;
my holding the door, her crossing the fragmented tiles, faltering at
    the step to the street,
droning, not looking at me, "Can you help me?" taking my arm,
    leaning lightly against me;
her wavering step into the world, her whispering, "Thanks, love,"
    lightly, lightly against me.

❖ TRAVELERS

He drives, she mostly sleeps; when she's awake, they quarrel, and
  now, in a violet dusk,
a rangy, raw-boned, efficient-looking mongrel loping toward
  them down the other shoulder
for no apparent reason swerves out on the roadbed just as a
  battered taxi is going by.
Horrible how it goes under, how it's jammed into the asphalt,
  compressed, abraded, crumpled,
then, ejected out behind, still, a miracle, alive, spins wildly on
  itself, tearing,
frenzied, at its broken spine, the mindless taxi driver never
  slowing, never noticing or caring,
they slowing, only for a moment, though, as, "Go on," she says, "go
  on, go on," face averted,
she can't look, while he, guilty as usual, fearful, fascinated and
  uncouth, can't not.

❖ SHAME

A girl who, in 1971, when I was living by myself, painfully lonely,
    bereft, depressed,
offhandedly mentioned to me in a conversation with some friends
    that although at first she'd found me—
I can't remember the term, some dated colloquialism signifying
    odd, unacceptable, out-of-things—
she'd decided that I was after all all right . . . years later she comes
    back to me from nowhere
and I realize that it wasn't my then irrepressible, unselective, in-
    cessant sexual want she meant,
which, when we'd been introduced, I'd naturally aimed at her and
    which she'd easily deflected,
but that she'd thought I really was, in myself, the way I looked and
    spoke and acted,
what she was saying, creepy, weird, whatever, and I am taken with
    a terrible humiliation.

❖ ON THE OTHER HAND

On the other hand, in Philadelphia, long ago, at a party on Camac
    Street on a Sunday afternoon,
a springtime or an early autumn Sunday afternoon, I know,
    though the occasion's lost
and whose house it was is even lost, near the party's end, a girl, a
    woman, someone else's wife,
a beauty, too, a little older than I was, an "older woman," elegant
    and admirable, and sober, too,
or nearly so, as I was coming down the stairs, put her hand on my
    hand on the landing,
caught me there and held me for a moment, with her hand, just
    her gentle hand, and with her look,
with how she looked at me, with some experience I didn't have,
    some delight I didn't understand,
and pulled me to her, and kissed me, hard, to let me taste what
    subtle lusts awaited me.

❖ THE DIRTY TALKER: D LINE, BOSTON

Shabby, tweedy, academic, he was old enough to be her father and
    I thought he was her father,
then realized he was standing closer than a father would so I
    thought he was her older lover.
And I thought at first that she was laughing, then saw it was more
    serious, more strenuous:
her shoulders spasmed back and forth; he was leaning close, his
    mouth almost against her ear.
He's terminating the affair, I thought: wife ill, the kids . . . the girl
    won't let him go.
We were in a station now, he pulled back half a head from her the
    better to behold her,
then was out the hissing doors, she sobbing wholly now so that
    finally I had to understand—
her tears, his grinning broadly in—at *me* now though, as though
    I were a portion of the story.

❖ THE MISTRESS

After the drink, after dinner, after the half-hour idiot kids' car-
    toon special on the TV,
after undressing his daughter, mauling at the miniature buttons
    on the back of her dress,
the games on the bed—"Look at my pee-pee," she says, pulling her
    thighs wide, "isn't it pretty?"—
after the bath, pajamas, the song and the kiss and telling his wife
    it's her turn now,
out now, at last, out of the house to make the call (out to take a
    stroll, this evening's lie),
he finds the only public phone booth in the neighborhood's been
    savaged, receiver torn away,
wires thrust back up the coin slot to its innards, and he stands
    there, what else? what now?
and notices he's panting, he's panting like an animal, he's
    breathing like a bloody beast.

❖ THE LOVER

When she stopped by, just passing, on her way back from picking
    up the kids at school,
taking them to dance, just happened by the business her husband
    owned and her lover worked in,
their glances, hers and the lover's, that is, not the husband's,
    seemed so decorous, so distant,
barely, just barely touching their fiery wings, their clanging she
    thought so well muffled,
that later, in the filthy women's bathroom, in the stall, she was
    horrified to hear two typists
coming from the office laughing, about them, all of them, their
    boss, her husband, "the blind pig,"
one said, and laughed, "and her, the horny bitch," the other said,
    and they both laughed again,
"and *him*, did you see *him*, that sanctimonious, lying bastard—I
    thought he was going to *blush*."

❖ VEHICLE

Conscience

That moment when the high-wire walker suddenly begins to
        falter, wobble, sway, arms flailing,
that breathtakingly rapid back-and-forth aligning-realigning of
        the displaced center of gravity,
weight thrown this way, no, too far; that way, no, too far again,
        until the movements themselves
of compensation have their rhythms established so that there's no
        way possibly to stop now . . .
that very moment, wheeling back and forth, back and forth,
        appeal, repeal, negation,
just before he lets it go and falls to deftly catch himself going by the
        wire, somersaulting up,
except for us it never ceases, testing moments of the mind-weight
        this way, back and back and forth,
no re-establishing of balance, no place to start again, just this, this
        force, this gravity and fear.

Forgetting

The way, playing an instrument, when you botch a passage you
        have to stop before you can go on again—
there's a chunk of time you have to wait through, an interval to let
        the false notes dissipate,
from consciousness of course, and from the muscles, but it seems
        also from the room, the actual air,

the bad try has to leak off into eternity, the volumes of being
  scrubbed to let the true resume . . .
so, having loved, and lost, lost everything, the other and the
  possibility of other and parts of self,
the heart rushes toward forgetfulness, but never gets there, con-
  tinuously attains the opposite instead,
the senses tensed, attending, the conductors of the mind alert,
  waiting for the waiting to subside:
when will tedious normality begin again, the old calm silences
  recur, the creaking air subside?

❖ TOIL

After the argument—argument? battle, war, harrowing; you need
      shrieks, moans from the pit—
after that woman and I anyway stop raking each other with the
      meathooks we've become with each other,
I fit my forehead into the smudge I've already sweated onto the
      window with a thousand other exhaustions
and watch an old man having breakfast out of a pile of bags on my
      front steps.
Peas from a can, bread with the day-old price scrawled over the
      label in big letters
and then a bottle that looks so delectable, the way he carefully
      unsheathes it
so the neck just lips out of the wrinkled foreskin of the paper and
      closes his eyes and tilts,
long and hard, that if there were one lie left in me to forgive a last
      rapture of cowardice
I'd go down there too and sprawl and let the whole miserable rest
      go to pieces.
Does anyone still want to hear how love can turn rotten?
How you can be so desperate that even going adrift wouldn't be
      enough—
you want to scour yourself out, get rid of all the needs you've still
      got in yourself
that keep you endlessly tearing against yourself in rages of guilt
      and frustration?
I don't. I'd rather think about other things. Beauty. How do you
      learn to believe there's beauty?

The kids going by on their way to school with their fat little lunch
      bags: beauty!

My old drunk with his bags—bottle bags, rag bags, shoe bags:
      beauty! beauty!

He lies there like the goddess of wombs and first-fruit, asleep in
      the riches,

one hand still hooked in mid-flight over the intricacies of the iron
      railing.

Old father, wouldn't it be a good ending if you and I could just
      walk away together?

Or that you were the king who reveals himself, who folds back the
      barbed, secret wings

and we're all so in love now, one spirit, one flesh, one generation,
      that the truces don't matter?

Or maybe a better ending would be that there is no ending.

Maybe the Master of Endings is wandering down through his
      herds to find it

and the cave cow who tells truth and the death cow who holds sea
      in her eyes are still there

but all he hears are the same old irresistible slaughter-pen bawl-
      ings.

So maybe there is no end to the story and maybe there's no story.

Maybe the last calf just ambles up to the trough through the
      clearing

and nudges aside the things that swarm on the water and her
      mouth dips in among them and drinks.

Then she lifts, and it pours, everything, gushes, and we're lost in
      both waters.

❖ EXPERIENCE

After a string of failed romances and intensely remarked sexual
    adventures she'd finally married.
The husband was a very formal man, handsome, elegant . . .
    perhaps to my taste too much so;
I sensed too much commitment in him to a life entailing . . .
    handsomeness and elegance, I suppose,
but he was generous with her and even their frequent arguments
    had a manageable vehemence.
She smiled often in those days, but behind her face an edge of
    animation seemed nailed shut.
You wouldn't really worry for her, by now you knew she'd be all
    right, but there were moments
when for no reason you could put your finger on you'd feel some-
    thing in yourself too rigidly attentive:
it was as though some soft herd-alarm, a warning signal from the
    species, had been permanently tripped.

❖ ANGER

I killed the bee for no reason except that it was there and you were
　　　watching, disapproving,
which made what I would do much worse but I was angry with
　　　you anyway and so I put my foot on it,
leaned on it, tested how much I'd need to make that resilient,
　　　resisting cartridge give way
and *crack!* abruptly, shockingly it did give way and you turned
　　　sharply and sharply now
I felt myself balanced in your eyes—why should I feel myself so
　　　balanced always in your eyes;
isn't just this half the reason for my rage, these tendencies of
　　　yours, susceptibilities of mine?—
and "Why?" your eyes said, "Why?" and even as mine sent back my
　　　answer, "None of your affair,"
I knew that I was being once again, twice now, weighed, and this
　　　time anyway found wanting.

❖ DREAM

Strange that one's deepest split from oneself
should be enacted in those banal and inevitable
productions of the double dark of sleep.
Despite all my broodings about dream,
I never fail to be amazed by the misery
I inflict on myself when I'm supposedly at rest.

Rest? In last night's dream my beloved announced to me,
and to others in the dream as well, that her desire was . . .
to not limit her range of sexual choice.
I implored her, but she wouldn't respond.
Why would characters in one's own dream
share with the waking world such awful unknowability?

Dreams are said to enact unfulfilled needs,
discords we can't admit to ourselves,
but I've never been able to believe that.
I dream pain, dream grief, dream shame,
I cry out, wake in terror:
is there something in me that *requires* such torment?

There used to be books of dream:
every dream had symbolic meaning.
And the old Chinese believed
that dreams implied their reversal:
a dream of travel meant you'd stay home,
to dream of death meant longer life.

Yes, yes! Surely my beloved in my dream
was saying she loved only me.
The coolness in your eyes, love, was really heat,
your wish to range was your renewal of allegiance;
those prying others were you and I ourselves,
beholding one another's fealty, one another's fire.

Mad dreams! Mad love!

❖ THE GAME

"Water" was her answer and I fell instantly and I knew self-
    destructively in love with her,
had to have her, would, I knew, someday, I didn't care how, and
    soon, too, have her,
though I guessed already it would have to end badly though not so
    disastrously as it did.

My answer, "lion" or "eagle," wasn't important: the truth would
    have been anything but myself.
The game of that first fateful evening was what you'd want to
    come back as after you died;
it wasn't the last life-or-death contest we'd have, only the least
    erotically driven and dangerous.

What difference if she was married, and perhaps mad (both only
    a little, I thought wrongly)?
There was only my jealous glimpse of her genius, then my vision
    of vengeance: midnight, morning—
beneath me a planet possessed: cycles of transfiguration and soar-
    ing, storms crossing.

❖ ONE OF THE MUSES

Nor will his vision of the beautiful take the form of a face, or of hands, or of anything that is of the flesh. It will be neither words, nor knowledge, nor a something that exists in something else, such as a living creature, or the earth, or the heavens, or anything that is . . .
   —Plato, *Symposium*

Where our language suggests a body and there is none: there we should like to say, is a spirit.
   —Wittgenstein, *Philosophical Investigations*

1.

I will not grace you with a name . . . Even "you," however modest
        the convention: not here.
No need here for that much presence. Let "you" be "she," and let
        the choice, incidentally,
be dictated not by bitterness or fear—a discretion, simply, the
        most inoffensive decorum.

This was, after all, if it needs another reason, long ago, and not just
        in monthly, yearly time,
not only in that house of memory events, the shadowed, off-sized
        rooms of which
it amuses us to flip the doors of like a deck of cards, but also in the
        much more malleable,

mazy, convoluted matter of the psyche itself, especially the
     wounded psyche,
especially the psyche stricken once with furrows of potential
     which are afterwards untenanted:
voids, underminings, to be buttressed with the webbiest filaments
     of day-to-dayness.

2.

Long ago, in another place, it seems sometimes in another realm
     of being altogether,
one of those dimensions we're told intersects our own, rests there
     side by side with ours,
liable to be punched across into by charity or prayer, other skul-
     lings at the muscle.

How much of her essential being can or should be carried over
     into now isn't clear to me.
that past which holds her, yellowed with allusiveness, is also
     charged with unreality:
a tiny theater in whose dim light one senses fearfully the contam-
     inating powers of illusion.

Here, in a relatively stable present, no cries across the gorge, no
     veils atremble,
it sometimes seems as though she may have been a fiction utterly,
     a symbol or a system of them.
In any case, what good conceivably could come at this late date of
     recapitulating my afflictions?

3.

Apparently, it would have to do with what that ancient desperation means to me today.

We recollect, call back, surely not to suffer; is there something then for me, today,

something lurking, potent with another loss, this might be meant to alter or avert?

No, emphatically: let it be that simple. And not any sort of longing backwards, either:

no desire to redeem defeats, no humiliations to atone for, no expiations or maledictions.

Why bother then? Why inflict it on myself again, that awful time, those vacillations and frustrations?

It's to be accounted for, that's all. Something happened, the time has come to find its place.

Let it just be that: not come to terms with, not salvage something from, not save.

There was this, it's to be accounted for: "she," for that, will certainly suffice.

4.

She had come to me . . . *She* to *me* . . . I know that, I knew it then, however much, at the end,

trying so to hang on to it, to keep something of what by then was nothing, I came to doubt,

to call the memory into question, that futile irreducible of what had happened and stopped happening.

(69)

She, to me, and with intensity, directness, aggression even, an
  aggression that may have been,
I think, the greater part of my involvement to begin with: in the
  sweep of her insistence,
it was as though she'd simply shouldered past some debilitating
  shyness on my part,

some misgiving, some lack of faith I'd never dared acknowledge in
  myself but which, now,
I suddenly understood had been a part of my most basic being: a
  tearing shoal of self,
which, brought to light now, harrowingly recognized, had flowed
  away beneath me.

5.

Later, when everything had turned, fallen, but when we still found
  ways, despite it all,
through our impediments—my grief, her ever-stricter panels of
  reserve—that first consummation,
her power, the surprising counter-power I answered with, came
  to seem a myth, a primal ceremony.

Later, and not much later because the start and end were, al-
  though I couldn't bear to think it,
nearly one, it became almost a ritual, not even ritual, a repetition,
  and I had to recognize,
at last, how few times that first real, unqualified soaring had
  actually been enacted.

Maybe several times, maybe only once: once and once—that
    would have been enough,
enough to keep me there, to keep me trying to recuperate it, so
    long after I'd begun to feel,
and to acknowledge to myself, her searing hesitations, falterings,
    awkwardnesses.

6.

Her withholdings were so indefinite at first, it wasn't hard to fend
    them off, deny them.
The gasp that seemed—but did it really?—to extend a beat into
    a sigh, and then the sigh,
did it go on an extra instant to become a heave of tedium, impa-
    tience, resignation?

… Then the silences: I could have, if I'd wanted to, dared to, been
    certain of the silences.
They were in time, had duration, could be measured: how I must
    have wanted not to know.
I didn't even name them that at first, "silence," no: lapses, inat-
    tentions, respites.

It feels as though I'd begun to try to cope with them before I'd
    actually remarked them.
They weren't silences until they'd flared and fused, until her
    silences became her silence,
until we seemed, to my chagrin, my anguish, horror, to be wholly
    in and of them.

7.

Her silence: how begin to speak of it? I think sometimes I must
   have simply gaped.
There were harmonies in it, progressions, colors, resolutions: it
   was a symphony, a tone poem.
I seemed to live in it, it was always with me, a matrix, background
   sound: surf, wind.

Sometimes, when I'd try to speak myself, I'd find it had insinuated
   into my voice:
it would haul at me; I'd go hoarse, metallic, hollow, nothing that
   I said entailed.
More and more her presence seemed preceded by it: a quiet on the
   stair, hushed hall.

I'd know before I heard her step that she was with me, and when
   she'd go, that other,
simpler silence, after all the rest, was like a coda, magnificent, ab-
   sorbing,
one last note reverberating on and on, subdividing through its
   physics toward eternity.

8.

At the same time, though, it was never, never quite, defined as
   being final.
She always, I have no idea how, left her clef of reticence ajar: a lace,
   a latticework.
I thought—I think that I was meant to think—it was provisional,
   a stopping place.

And, to exacerbate things, it became her: with it, and within it, she
　　seemed to promise more.
The sheer *focus* it demanded; such shadings were implied in how
　　she turned in it;
the subtleties I hadn't been allowed, the complexities not fath-
　　omed: she was being re-enhanced by it.

What was inaccessible in her, what not, what—even as I'd hold
　　her, even as we'd touch—
was being drawn away, marked off, forbidden: such resonance
　　between potential and achieved.
The vibrations, though, as subtle as they were, crystalline, were
　　tearing me apart.

9.

Sometimes, it would seem as though, still with me, she had al-
　　ready left me.
Sometimes, later, when she really had left, left again, I would seem
　　to ache,
not with the shocks or after-shocks of passion, but with simply
　　holding her, holding on.

Sometimes, so flayed, I would think that I was ready to accept
　　defeat, ready to concede.
I may have wished for hints of concrete evidence from her that she
　　wanted us to stop.
She could, I thought, with the gentlest move, have disengaged: I
　　was ready for it . . .

No, not so, I wasn't. Wasn't what was wrong so slight, so patently
    inconsequential to the rest?
If I let her go like that, I thought, how would I ever know that
    what had brought us down
wasn't merely my own dereliction or impatience? No, there had to
    be a way to solve this.

10.

I kept thinking: there is something which, if said in precisely the
    right words to her . . .
I kept thinking, there's an explanation I can offer, an analysis,
    maybe just a way of saying,
a rhythm or a rhetoric, to fuse the strands of her ambivalence and
    draw her back.

I kept thinking—she may have kept me thinking—there's some-
    thing I haven't understood about her,
something I've misconceived or misconstrued, something I've
    missed the message of and offended . . .
I'd set theories up from that, programs, and, with notes along the
    way toward future tries,

I'd elaborate the phrases, paragraphs, the volumes of my explica-
    tion: I'd rehearse them,
offer them, and have her, out of hand, hardly noticing, reject,
    discard, disregard them,
until I learned myself—it didn't take me long—out of hand,
    hardly noticing, to discard them.

11.

Sometimes, though, I'd imagine that something—yes—I'd said
	would reach her.
Her presence, suddenly, would seem to soften, there would be a
	flood of ease, a decontraction.
She'd be with me, silent still, but *there*, and I would realize how far
	she'd drifted.

I wouldn't know then, having her, or thinking that I did, whether
	to be miserable or pleased.
I'd go on, even so, to try to seal it, build on it, extend, certify it
	somehow,
and then, suddenly again, I'd sense that she'd be gone again, or,
	possibly, much worse,

had never been there, or not the way I'd thought it for that thank-
	ful instant,
I'd misinterpreted, misread, I'd have to start my search again, my
	trial, travail.
Where did I ever find the energy for it? Just to think about it now
	exhausts me.

12.

Wherever I did find the strength, half of it I dedicated to absolv-
	ing and forgiving her.
Somehow I came to think, and never stopped believing, I was
	inflicting all my anguish on myself.
She was blameless, wasn't she? Her passivity precluded else: the
	issue had to be with me.

I tried to reconceive myself, to situate myself in the syntax of our
    crippled sentence.
I parsed myself, searching out a different flow for the tangle of
    amputated phrases I was by then.
Nothing, though, would sound, would scan, no matter how I
    carved, dissected, chopped.

I couldn't find the form, the meter, rhythm, or, by now, the barest
    context for myself.
I became a modifier: my only function was to alter the conditions
    of this fevered predication.
I became a word one thinks about too closely: clumps of curves
    and serifs, the arbitrary symbol of itself.

13.

I became, I became . . . Finally, I think I must have simply ceased
    even that, becoming.
I was an image now, petrified, unmediated, with no particular
    association, no connotation,
certainly no meaning, certainly no hope of ever being anything
    that bore a meaning.

It was as though my identify had been subsumed in some enor-
    mous generalization,
one so far beyond my comprehension that all I could know was
    that I was incidental to it,
that with me or without me it would grind along the complex
    epicycles of its orbit.

It was as though the system I'd been living in had somehow suddenly evolved beyond me.
I had gills to breathe a stratosphere, and my hopeless project was to generate new organs,
new lobes to try to comprehend this emotional ecology, and my extinction in it.

14.

The hours, the labor: how I wracked my mind, how my mind revenged itself on me.
I was wild, helpless, incapable of anything at all by now but watching as I tore myself.
I huddled there at the center of myself and tried to know by some reflexive act of faith

that I'd survive all this, this thing, my self, that mauled and savaged me.
I'd behold it all, so much frenzy, so many groans and bellows; even now, watching now,
I seem to sink more deeply into some protective foliage: I tremble in here, quake,

and then I dart—even now, still, my eyes, despite me, dart: walls, floor, sky—
I dart across that field of fear, away, away from there, from here, from anywhere.
I was frightened sometimes that I might go mad. And then I did just that—go mad.

15.

It was like another mind, my madness, my blessèd, holy madness:
     no, it *was* another mind.
It arrives, my other mind, on another night when I'm without her,
     hoping, or past hope.
My new mind comes upon me with a hush, a fluttering, a silvery
     ado, and it has a volume,

granular and sensitive, which exactly fits the volume of the mind
     I already have.
Its desire seems to be to displace that other mind, and something
     in me—how say what?
how explain the alacrity of such a radical concurrence?—decides
     to let it,

and the split second of the decision and the onset of the workings
     of that mind are instantaneous.
In one single throb of intuition I understood what the function of
     my mind was,
because, in and of it now, convinced, absorbed, I was already
     working out its implications.

16.

I knew already that my other mind—I hardly could recall it—had
     had a flaw and from that flaw
had been elaborated a delusion, and that delusion in its turn was
     at the base of all my suffering,
all the agonies I'd been inflicting, so unnecessarily, I understood,
     upon myself.

I had thought, I realized, that reality of experience, data and
    events, were to be received,
that perception, sensory, experiential accumulation, was essen-
    tially passive,
that it accepted what was offered and moved within that given, the
    palpable or purely mental,

partaking of it as it could, jiggling the tenuous impressions here or
    there a bit,
a sentence added, or a chapter, but nothing more than that: we
    were almost victims,
or if not victims quite, not effective agents surely, not of anything
    that mattered.

17.

What my new mind made me understand, though the facts had
    been there all the while before my eyes,
was that reality, as I'd known it, as I knew it now, was being gener-
    ated, every second,
out of me and by me: it was me, myself, and no one else, who spun
    it out this way.

It was my own will, unconscious until now but now with purpose
    and intent, which made the world.
Not made-up, which implies imagination or idea, but made,
    actually created, everything,
in a flow, a logic, a succession of events, I could trace now with my
    very blood.

Even time: looking back at the wash of time on earth, it, too, was
     a function of this moment.
Then cosmic time was flowing, too, from the truth I was living
     now, not for myself now,
for my salvation or survival, but for the infinitely vulnerable fact of
     existence itself.

18.

Does it matter very much what the rest was, the odd conclusions
     I kept coming to?
What really seems important was that even as it happened, even
     as I let it happen,
even as I held it in a sort of mental gale—it wasn't necessary then
     to work it out like this,

all of it was there at once, in a single block, entire, a kind of geo-
     metric bliss—
I understood that it was all hallucination and delusion, that these
     insights or illuminations
were wretched figments of emotion all, but I didn't care, I let them
     take me further,

past proposition, syllogism, sense: I was just a premise mechanism
     now, an epistemology machine;
I let my field of vision widen—everything was mine now, coal and
     comet, root and moon,
all found their footing, fulfilled at last, in my felicity, and then,
     rendingly, it ended.

19.

Why it stopped was as much a mystery to me as why it should
     have happened in the first place,
but when it did, something else took its place, a sort of vision, or
     a partial vision,
or at least a knowledge, as instantly accessible and urgent as the
     other, and, I'd find, as fleeting.

Somehow, I knew, I'd touched into the very ground of self, its
     axioms and assumptions,
and what was there wasn't what I'd thought—I hadn't *known*
     what I'd thought but knew it now—
not violence, not conflagration, sexual turbulence, a philosophic
     or emotive storm,

but a sort of spiritual erasure, a nothingness of motive and inten-
     tion, and I understood, too,
in another bolt, that all that keeps us from that void, paradoxically
     perhaps, is trust . . .
Trust in what? Too late: that perception, too, was gone; I had to
     watch another revelation end.

20.

But not badly, even so . . . I came back, to myself, feeling not
     contrite, not embarrassed,
certainly not frightened . . . awkward, maybe, toward myself, shy,
     abashed: I couldn't, as it were,
meet the gaze of this stranger I was in a body with, but I couldn't,
     either, take my eyes away.

Something had altered, *I* had: there was something unfamiliar,
    incongruous about me.
I couldn't specify exactly, not at first, what I felt; it wasn't, though,
    unpleasant.
I probed myself as though I'd had an accident; nothing broken, I
    was all right, more:

a sense of lightness, somehow, a change in my specific gravity, a
    relief, unburdening,
and then I knew, with no fuss or flourish, what it was: she, she
    wasn't with me now,
she was gone from me, from either of my minds, all my minds, my
    selves—she simply wasn't there.

21.

I could say it feels as though I'm taking breaths: she is gone and
    gone, he, shriven of her,
leaps into his life, but as I went about the work of understanding
    what had happened to me,
who I was now, it was clear at once that my having torn myself
    from her was unimportant.

She was gone, why she'd been there to begin with, what I'd seen in
    her, thought she'd meant,
why I'd let that suffering come to me, became immediately the
    most theoretical of questions.
That I'd have to be without her now meant only that: without her,
    not forlorn, bereft.

I even tested cases: if she went on to someone else, touched some-
    one else, would I envy them,
her touch, her fire? Not even that: her essence for me was her
    being with me for that time,
with someone else, she, too, was other than herself: a wraith, a
    formula or intellection.

22.

I felt no regret—indifference, rather, a flare of disbelief, then an
    unexpected moment of concern.
Had she suffered, too? Had she even sensed, in her empyrean
    distance, that this,
any of it, was going on at all? I didn't answer then, if I had to now,
    I'd have to doubt it.

I think that, after those first moments, she was gone already from
    me: perhaps, though,
it's not my task to try to answer, perhaps all I really have the right
    to do is ask
what the person I am now might have to do with her, wraith or
    not, memory of a memory or not?

Was I enhanced by her? Diminished by her? All that's really sure
    is that if I was changed,
it wasn't the embrace, the touch, that would have done it, but
    what came after, her withdrawal,
her painful non-responses, her absence and the ever more incor-
    poreal innuendos in that absence.

23.

And my "madness," that business of the other mind, that "trust":
    have I taken anything from that?
Perhaps. I think I'd always realized the possibility was there for
    us to do that to ourselves,
undo ourselves that way, not in suicide, but in something much
    more dire, complete, denying.

I think that I'd suspected, too, that with the means to do it, I
    would someday have to do it.
And now, what I'd been afraid I'd do, I'd done: that she'd had to
    drive me to it didn't matter,
although probably without her, without what she'd inflicted on
    me, I'd have never come to it.

Perhaps, with her abrasive offerings and takings-back, I'd been
    ground down like a lens:
I'd had, to my horror, really to look within myself, into the
    greater sea of chaos there,
and I'd survived it, shaken but intact, with auras, even, of a kind
    of gratitude.

24.

What I'm left with after all this time is still the certainty that
    something was attained,
though all that remain now are flickers, more and more occa-
    sional, more disjointed—
pale remnants of the harsh collaborations those intermediary
    silences symbolized so well.

(84)

And this . . . I mean *this*, these lines, constructions, études: these
    small histories,
where did this come from? As I said, there was no desire to go over
    all of it again,
but, after all, whatever ambivalence I felt about it, it demanded
    care, even labor.

The need for doing it never quite defined itself: it, like her, came
    uncalled for.
A tone took me, an impulse toward a structure: I found it inter-
    esting, a question of aesthetics.
If that were so, might there be another way, another mode in
    which to come to it?

25.

The proposition now could be that this *is* she, this, itself, wholly
    "she."
Not an artifact, not a net in which some wingèd thing protests or
    pines, but her,
completely fused now, inspiration, outcome: she would be, now,
    what she herself effected,

the tones themselves, the systems she wrought from the conflict-
    ing musics of my conscience.
This time it would be that all she meant to me were these at-
    tempts, these uncertain colorations,
that took so long to get here, from so far, and from which she
    would be departing now at last,

(85)

not into another hesitation, pause, another looking back reluc-
    tantly on either of our parts—
no turnings, no farewells—but a final sundering, a seeing-off, a
    last, definitely indicated,
precisely scored—no rests, diminuendos, decrescendos—silenc-
    ing, and silence.

❖ SONG

A city square, paths empty, sky clear; after days of rain, a purified
    sunlight blazed through;
all bright, all cool, rinsed shadows all vivid; the still-dripping
    leaves sated, prolific.

Suddenly others: voices, anger; sentences started, aborted; harsh,
    honed hisses of fury:
two adults, a child, the grown-ups raging, the child, a girl, seven or
    eight, wide-eyed, distracted.

"You, you," the parents boiled on in their clearly eternal battle:
    "you creature, you cruel,"
and the child stood waiting, instead of going to play on the slide or
    the swing, stood listening.

I wished she would weep; I could imagine the rich, abashing gush
    springing from her:
otherwise mightn't she harden her heart; mightn't she otherwise
    without knowing it become scar?

But the day was still perfect, the child, despite her evident appre-
    hension, slender, exquisite:
when she noticed me watching, she precociously, flirtily, fetch-
    ingly swept back her hair.

Yes, we know one another, yes, there in the sad broken music of
    mind where nothing is lost.
Sorrow, love, they were so sweetly singing: *where shall I refuge seek if*
    you refuse me?

III. YOU

❖ A DREAM OF MIND: YOU

Such longing, such urging, such warmth towards, such force to-
    wards, so much ardor and desire;
to touch, touch into, hold, hold against, to feel, feel against and
    long towards again,
as though the longing, urge, and warmth were ends in themselves,
    the increase of themselves,
the force towards, the ardor and desire, focused, increased, the
    incarnation of themselves.
All this in the body of dream, all in the substance of dream; allure,
    attraction, and need,
the force so consumed and rapt in its need that dream might have
    evolved it from itself,
except the ardor urges always towards the other, towards you, and
    without you it decays,
becomes vestige, reflex, the defensive attempt to surmount instinc-
    tual qualms and misgivings.
No qualms now, no misgivings; no hesitance or qualifications in
    longing towards you;
no frightened wish to evolve ideals to usurp qualm, fear or misgiv-
    ing, not any longer.
The longing towards you sure now, ungeneralized, certain, the urge
    now towards you in yourself,
your own form of nearness, the surface of desire multiplied in the
    need that urges from you,
your longing, your urging, the force and the warmth from you, the
    sure ardor blazing in you.

❖ THE BED

Beds squalling, squealing, muffled in hush; beds pitching, leap-
　　ing, immobile as mountains;
beds wide as a prairie, strait as a gate, as narrow as the plank of a
　　ship to be walked.

*I squalled, I squealed, I swooped and pitched; I covered my eyes and fell
　　from the plank.*

Beds proud, beds preening, beds timid and tense; vanquished beds
　　wishing only to vanquish;
neat little beds barely scented and dented, beds so disused you
　　cranked them to start them.

*I admired, sang praises, flattered, adored; I sighed and submitted, solaced,
　　comforted, cranked.*

Procrustean beds with consciences sharpened like razors slicing
　　the darkness above you;
beds like the labors of Hercules, stables and serpents; Samson
　　blinded, Noah in horror.

*Blind with desire, I wakened in horror, in toil, in bondage, my conscience
　　in tatters.*

Beds sobbing, beds sorry, beds pleading, beds mournful with his-
　　tories that amplified yours,
so you knelled through their dolorous echoes as through the depths
　　of your own dementias.

I echoed, I knelled, I sobbed and repented, I bandaged the wrists, sighed for
    embryos lost.

A nation of beds, a cosmos, then, how could it still happen, the
    bed at the end of the world,
as welcoming as the world, ark, fortress, light and delight, the other
    beds all forgiven, forgiving.

A bed that sang through the darkness and woke in song as though world
    itself had just wakened;
two beds fitted together as one; bed of peace, patience, arrival, bed of
    unwaning ardor.

❖ WITH IGNORANCE

With ignorance begins a knowledge the first characteristic of which is igno-
rance.
        —Kierkegaard

1.

Again and again. Again lips, again breast, again hand, thigh, loin
        and bed and bed
after bed, the hunger, hunger again, need again, the rising, the
        spasm and needing again.
Flesh, lie, confusion and loathing, the scabs of clear gore, the spent
        seed and the spurt
of desire that seemed to generate from itself, from its own rising
        and spasm.
Everything waste, everything would be or was, the touching, the
        touch and the touch back.
Everything rind, scar, without sap, without meaning or seed, and
        everyone, everyone else,
every slip or leap into rage, every war, flame, sob, it was there, too,
        the stifling, the hushed,
malevolent frenzy and croak of desire, again and again, the same
        hunger, same need.
Touch me, hold me, sorrow and sorrow, the emptied, emptied again,
        touched again.
The hunger, the rising, again and again until again itself seemed
        to be need and hunger
and so much terror could rise out of that, the hunger repeating
        itself out of the fear now,

that how could you know if you lived within it at all, if there wasn't
    another,
a malediction or old prayer, a dream or a city of dream or a single,
    fleshless, dreamless error,
whose tongue you were, who spoke with you, butted or rasped
    with you, but still, tongue or another,
word or not word, what could it promise that wouldn't drive us
    back to the same hunger and sorrow?
What could it say that wouldn't spasm us back to ourselves to be
    bait or a dead prayer?
Or was that it? Only that? The prayer hunting its prey, hunting
    the bait of itself?
Was the hunger the faith in itself, the belief in itself, even the
    prayer?
Was it the dead prayer?

2.

The faces waver; each gathers the others within it, the others shud-
    dering through it
as though there were tides or depths, as though the depths, the
    tides of the eyes themselves
could throw out refractions, waves, shifts and wavers and each
    faceless refraction
could rise to waver beneath me, to shift, to be faceless again, be-
    neath or within me,
the lying, confusion, recurrence, reluctance, the surge through into
    again.
Each room, each breast finding its ripeness of shadow, each lip
    and its shadow,

the dimming, flowing, the waver through time, through loss, gone, irredeemable,

all of it, each face into regret, each room into forgetting and absence.

But still, if there were a moment, still, one moment, to begin in or go back to,

to return to move through, waver through, only a single moment carved back from the lie

the way the breast is carved from its shadow, sealed from the dross of darkness

until it takes the darkness itself and fills with it, taking the breath;

if, in the return, I could be taken the way I could have been taken, with voice or breast,

emptied against the space of the breast as though breast was breath and my breath,

taken, would have been emptied into the moment, it could rise here, now, in that moment, the same moment.

But it won't, doesn't. The moments lift and fall, break, and it shifts, wavers,

subsides into the need again, the faceless again, the faceless and the lie.

3.

Remorse? Blame? There is a pit-creature. The father follows it down with the ax.

Exile and sorrow. Once there were things we lived in, don't you remember?

We scraped, starved, then we came up, abashed, to the sun, and what was the first word?

Blame, blame and remorse, then sorrow, then the blame was the
    father then was ourselves.
Such a trite story, do we have to retell it? The mother took back
    the sun and we . . .
Remorse, self-regard, call it shame or being abashed or trying again,
    for the last time, to return.
Remorse, then power, the power and the blame and what did we
    ever suffer but power?
The head lifting itself, then the wars, remorse and revenge, the
    wars of humility,
the blades and the still valley, the double intention, the simple tree
    in the blood.
The exile again, even the sword, even the spear, the formula
    scratched on the sand,
even the christening, the christened, blame again, power again,
    but even then,
taken out of the fire at the core and never returned, what could we
    not sanction?
One leg after the other, the look back, the power, the fire again
    and the sword again.
Blame and remorse. That gives into desire again, into hunger again.
    That gives into . . . this . . .

4.

Someone . . . Your arm touches hers or hers finds yours, unmov-
    ing, unasking.
A silence, as though for the first time, and as though for the first
    time, you can listen,
as though there were chords: your life, then the other's, someone
    else, as though for the first time.

The life of the leaves over the streetlamp and the glow, swelling,
    chording, under the shadows,
and the quaver of things built, one quavering cell at a time, and
    the song
of the cell gently bedding itself in its mortar, in this silence, this
    first attempting.
Even the shush of cars, the complex stress of a step, the word called
    into the darkness,
and, wait, the things even beyond, beyond membrane or aware-
    ness, mode, sense, dream,
don't they sing, too? Chord, too? Isn't the song and the silence
    there, too?
I heard it once. It changed nothing, but once, before I went on, I
    did hear:
the equation of star and plant, the wheel, the ecstasy and division,
    the equation again.
The absolute walking its planks, its long wall, its long chord of
    laughter or grief.
I heard silence, then the children, the spawn, how we have to teach
    every cell how to speak,
and from that, after that, the kiss back from the speech, the touch
    back from the song.
And then more, I heard how it alters, how we, the speakers, the
    can't-live, the refuse-to,
how we, only in darkness, groaning and thrashing into the under-
    growth of our eternal,
would speak then, would howl, howl again, and at last, at the end,
    we'd hear it:
the prayer and the flesh crying *Why aren't you here?* And the cry
    back in it, *I am! I am!*

5.

Imagine dread. Imagine, without symbol, without figure, history
or histories; a place, not a place.
Imagine it must be risen through, beginning with the silent mo-
ment, the secrets quieted,
one hour, one age at a time, sadness, nostalgia, the absurd pain of
betrayal.
Through genuine grief, then through the genuine suffering for the
boundaries of self
and the touch on the edge, the compassion, that never, never quite,
breaks through.
Imagine the touch again and beyond it, beyond either end, joy or
terror, either ending,
the context that gives way, not to death, but past, past anything
still with a name,
even death, because even death is a promise offering comfort, so-
lace, that any direction we turn,
there'll still be the word, the name, and this the promise now, even
with terror,
the promise again that the wordlessness and the self won't be for
one instant the same enacting,
and we stay within it, a refusal now, a turning away, a never giving
way,
we stay until even extinction itself, the absence, death itself, even
death, isn't longed for,
never that, but turned toward in the deepest turn of the self, the
deepest gesture toward self.
And then back, from the dread, from locution and turn, from
whatever history reflects us,

the self grounds itself again in itself and reflects itself, even its
    loss, as its own,

and back again, still holding itself back, the certainty and belief
    tearing again,

back from the edge of that one flood of surrender which, given
    space, would, like space itself,

rage beyond any limit, the flesh itself giving way in its terror, and
    back from that,

into love, what we have to call love, the one moment before we
    move onwards again,

toward the end, the life again of the self-willed, self-created, em-
    bodied, reflected again.

Imagine a space prepared for with hunger, with dread, with power
    and the power

over dread which is dread, and the love, with no space for itself, no
    power for itself,

a moment, a silence, a rising, the terror for that, the space for that.
    Imagine love.

6.

Morning. The first morning of now. You, your touch, your song
    and morning, but still,

something, a last fear or last lie or last clench of confusion clings,

holds back, refuses, resists, the way fear itself clings in its web of
    need or dread.

What would release be? Being forgiven? No, never forgiven, never
    only forgiven.

To be touched, somehow, with presence, so that the only sign is a
    step, towards or away?

Or not even a step, because the walls, of self, of dread, can never
release,

can never forgive stepping away, out of the willed or refused, out
of the lie or the fear

of the self that still holds back and refuses, resists, and turns back
again and again into the willed.

What if it could be, though? The first, hectic rush past guilt or
remorse?

What if we could find a way through the fires that aren't with us
and the terrors that are?

What would be there? Would we be thrown back into perhaps or
not yet or not needed or done?

Could we even slip back, again, past the first step into the first
refusal,

the first need, first blot of desire that still somehow exists and
wants to resist, wants to give back the hard,

immaculate shell of the terror it still keeps against respite and
unclenching?

Or perhaps no release, no step or sign, perhaps only to wait and
accept.

Perhaps only to bless. To bless and to bless and to bless and to
bless.

Willed or unwilled, word or sign, the word suddenly filled with
its own breath.

Self and other the self within other and the self still moved through
its word,

consuming itself, still, and consuming, still being rage, war, the
fear, the aghast,

but bless, bless still, even the fear, the loss, the gutting of word, the
gutting even of hunger,

but still to bless and bless, even the turn back, the refusal, to bless
   and to bless and to bless.

7.

The first language was loss, the second sorrow, this is the last,
   then: yours . . .
An island, summer, late dusk; hills, laurel and thorn. I walked from
   the harbor, over the cliff road,
down the long trail through the rocks. When I came to our house
   the ship's wake was just edging onto the shore
and on the stone beach, under the cypress, the low waves reas-
   suming themselves in the darkness, I waited.
There was a light in a room. You came to it, leaned to it, reaching,
   touching,
and watching you, I saw you give back to the light a light more
   than light
and to the silence you gave more than silence, and, in the silence, I
   heard it.
You, your self, your life, your beginning, pleasure, song clear as the
   light that touched you.
Your will, your given and taken: grief, recklessness, need, or de-
   sire.
Your passion or tear, step forward or step back into the inevitable
   veil.
Yours and yours and yours, the dream, the wall of the self that
   won't be or needn't be breached,
and the breach, the touch, yours and the otherness, yours, the sepa-
   rateness,
never giving way, never breached really, but as simple, always, as
   light, as silence.

This is the language of that, that light and that silence, the silence
     rising through or from you.
Nothing to bless or not bless now, nothing to thank or forgive, not
     to triumph,
surrender, mean, reveal, assume or exhaust. Our faces bent to the
     light, and still,
there is terror, still history, power, grief and remorse, always, al-
     ways the self and the other
and the endless tide, the waver, the terror again, between and be-
     neath, but you, now,
your touch, your light, the otherness yours, the reach, the wheel,
     the waves touching.
And to, not wait, not overcome, not even forget or forgive the dream
     of the moment, the unattainable moment again.
Your light . . . Your silence . . .
In the silence, without listening, I heard it, and without words,
     without language or breath, I answered.

❖ FRIENDS

My friend Dave knew a famous writer who used to have screw-
    drivers for breakfast.
He'd start with half gin and half juice and the rest of the day he'd
    sit with the same glass
in the same chair and add gin. The drink would get paler and
    paler, finally he'd pass out.
Every day was the same. Sometimes, when I'm making milk for
    the baby, cutting the thick,
sweet formula from the can with sterilized water, the baby, hun-
    gry again, still hungry,
rattling his rickety, long-legged chair with impatience, I think of
    that story.
Dave says the writer could talk like a god. He'd go on for hours in
    the same thought.
In his books, though, you never find out why he drove so hard
    toward his death.
I have a death in my memory that lately the word itself always
    brings back. I'm not quite sure why.
A butterfly, during a downpour one afternoon, hooked onto my
    screen. I thought it was waiting.
The light was just so. Its eyes caught the flare so it seemed to be
    watching me in my bed.
When I got up to come closer and it should have been frightened,
    it hung on.
After the rain, it was still there. Its eyes were still shining. I touched
    the screen
and it fell to the ledge. There were blue streaks on its wings. A
    while later, the wind took it.

The writer drowned in his puke or his liver exploded—it depends on the story.

He was a strong man, for all that. He must have thought it was taking forever.

Dave says when he'd wake with amnesia, he wouldn't want you to fill in the gaps.

He just wanted his gin and his juice. From all that you hear, he was probably right.

When we were young and we'd drink our minds to extinction, that was the best part: you did this, you said that.

It was like hearing yourself in a story. Sometimes real life is almost the same,

as though you were being recited; you can almost tell what a thought is before it arrives.

When I follow my mind now, another butterfly happens. It's not hard to see why.

It's the country this time. The butterfly walked over the white table and onto my hand.

I lifted it and it held. My friends were amazed. Catherine tried, too, but the butterfly fluttered away.

I put my hand back in the air and it found me again. It came down on a finger and clung.

Its sails listed. I could see it untwirling the barb of its tongue on my nail. I shook it away.

Those were the days and the nights when Catherine and I were first falling in love.

Sometimes, in the dark, I'd still be afraid but she'd touch my arm and I'd sleep.

The visions I had then were all death: they were hideous and absurd and had nothing to do with my life.

All I feel now about death is a sadness, not to be here with every-
one I love,
but in those days, I'd dream, I'd be wracked, Catherine would have
to reach over to hold me.
In the morning, it would be better. Even at dawn, when I'd wake
first, trembling, gasping for air,
I'd burrow back down, Catherine would open her eyes, smiling,
with me at her breast, and it would be better.

❖ MORNINGS: CATHERINE

Sometimes she'd begin to sing to herself before she was out of
     bed, before, I can remember thinking
as I listened from my table in the other room, she really could
     have even been all the way awake:
no sound of sheets pulled back, footsteps, just her voice, her song,
     so soft at first I wasn't sure,
rising from the silence but so close to being in it still that I couldn't
     hear the words,
only the threads of melody a car passing or a child crying in an-
     other house would brush away,
until it would insist again, or I'd think it would, with the volume
     of a breeze, the odor of a breeze . . .
Waiting to hear it again, to hear her again, I wouldn't move, I'd
     almost, yes, hold my breath:
her voice, her song, the meshings and unmeshings with the at-
     tending world, with my incredulity.

❖ DEPTHS

I'm on a parapet looking down
into a deep cleft in the earth
at minuscule people and cars
moving along its narrow bottom.
Though my father's arms are around me
I feel how far it would be to fall,
how perilous: I cringe back,
my father holds me more tightly.
Was there ever such a crevice?
No, I realized much, much later
we were on an ordinary building
looking down into a city street.

A picture book: desert sunlight,
a man and woman clad in sandals,
pastel robes, loose burnooses,
plying a material like dough,
the man kneading in a trough,
the woman throwing at a wheel.
Somehow I come to think they're angels,
in heaven, fashioning human beings.
Was there ever such a story?
No, the book, at Sunday school,
showed daily life in the Bible,
the people were just making jars.

Just jars, and yet those coils of clay,
tinted light to dark like skin,
swelled beneath the woman's hands
as I knew already flesh should swell,
and as I'd know it later, when,
alone with someone in the dark,
I'd close my eyes, move my hands
across her, and my mouth across her,
trying to experience an ideal,
to participate in radiances
I passionately believed existed,
and not only in imagination.

Or, with love itself, the love
that came to me so readily, so
intensely, so convincingly each time,
and each time ravaged me
when it spoiled and failed, and left
me only memories of its promise.
Could real love ever come to me?
Would I distort it if it did?
Even now I feel a frost of fear
to think I might not have found you,
my love, or not believed in you,
and still be reeling on another roof.

❖ SNOW: I

All night, snow, then, near dawn, freezing rain, so that by morn-
ing the whole city glistens
in a glaze of high-pitched, meticulously polished brilliance, every-
thing rounded off,
the cars submerged nearly to their windows in the unbroken drifts
lining the narrow alleys,
the buildings rising from the trunklike integuments the wind has
molded against them.
Underlit clouds, blurred, violet bars, the rearguard of the storm,
still hang in the east,
immobile over the flat river basin of the Delaware; beyond them,
nothing, the washed sky,
one vivid wisp of pale smoke rising waveringly but emphatically
into the brilliant ether.
No one is out yet but Catherine, who closes the door behind her
and starts up the street.

❖ SNOW: II

It's very cold, Catherine is bundled in a coat, a poncho on top of
    that, high boots, gloves,
a long scarf around her neck, and she's sauntering up the middle
    of the snowed-in street,
eating, of all things, an apple, the blazing redness of which shocks
    against the world of white.
No traffic yet, the *crisp crisp* of her footsteps keeps reaching me
    until she turns the corner.
I write it down years later, and the picture still holds perfectly,
    precise, unwanting,
and so too does the sense of being suddenly bereft as she passes
    abruptly from my sight,
the quick wash of desolation, the release again into the memory of
    affection, and then affection,
as the first trucks blundered past, chains pounding, the first de-
    lighted children rushed out with sleds.

❖ PEACE

We fight for hours, through dinner, through the endless evening,
    who even knows now what about,
what could be so dire to have to suffer so for, stuck in one another's
    craws like fishbones,
the cadavers of our argument dissected, flayed, but we go on with
    it, to bed, and through the night,
feigning sleep, dreaming sleep, hardly sleeping, so precisely never
    touching, back to back,
the blanket bridged across us for the wintry air to tunnel down, to
    keep us lifting, turning,
through the angry dark that holds us in its cup of pain, the aching
    dark, the weary dark,
then, toward dawn, I can't help it, though justice won't I know be
    served, I pull her to me,
and with such accurate, graceful deftness she rolls to me that we
    arrive embracing our entire lengths.

❖ THE CAVE

I think most people are relieved the first time they actually know
    someone who goes crazy.
It doesn't happen the way you hear about it where the person gib-
    bers and sticks to you like an insect:
mostly there's crying, a lot of silence, sometimes someone will
    whisper back to their voices.
All my friend did was sit, at home until they found him, then for
    hours at a time on his bed in the ward,
pointing at his eyes, chanting the same phrase over and over. "Too
    much fire!" he'd say. "Too much fire!"
I remember I was amazed at how raggedy he looked, then an-
    noyed because he wouldn't answer me
and then, when he was getting better, I used to pester him to tell
    me about that fire-thing.
He'd seemed to be saying he'd seen too much and I wanted to
    know too much what
because my obsession then was that I was somehow missing ev-
    erything beyond the ordinary.
What was only real was wrong. There were secrets that could turn
    you into stone,
they were out of range or being kept from me, but my friend, if he
    knew what I meant, wouldn't say,
so we'd talk politics or books or moon over a beautiful girl who
    was usually in the visiting room when we were
who mutilated herself. Every time I was there, new slashes would've
    opened out over her forearms and wrists
and once there were two brilliant medallions on her cheeks that I
    thought were rouge spots

but that my friend told me were scratches she'd put there with a
broken light bulb when she'd run away the day before.

The way you say running away in hospitals is "eloping." Someone
who hurts themself is a "cutter."

How could she do it to herself? My friend didn't think that was
the question.

She'd eloped, cut, they'd brought her back and now she was wait-
ing there again,

those clowny stigmata of lord knows what on her, as tranquil and
seductive as ever.

I used to storm when I'd leave her there with him. She looked so
vulnerable.

All the hours they'd have. I tormented myself imagining how they'd
come together,

how they'd tell each other the truths I thought I had to under-
stand to live,

then how they'd kiss, their lips, chaste and reverent, rushing over
the forgiven surfaces.

Tonight, how long afterwards, watching my wife undress, letting
my gaze go so everything blurs

but the smudges of her nipples and hair and the wonderful lumpy
graces of her pregnancy,

I still can bring it back: those dismal corridors, the furtive rods,
the moans I thought were sexual

and the awful lapses that seemed vestiges of exaltations I would
never have,

but now I know whatever in the mystery I was looking for, what-
ever brute or cloud I thought eluded me,

isn't lost in the frenzy of one soul or another, but next to us, in the
touch, between.

(114)

Lying down, fumbling for the light, moving into the shadow with
my son or daughter, I find it again:
the prism of hidden sorrow, the namelessness of nothing and noth-
ing shuddering across me,
and then the warmth, clinging and brightening, the hide, the caul,
the first mind.

My father-in-law is away, Catherine and I and Renée, her mother,
    are eating in the kitchen;
Jed, three weeks old, sleeps in his floppy straw cradle on the counter
    next to the bread box;
we've just arrived, and I'm so weary with jet lag, with the labor of
    tending to a newborn
that my mind drifts and, instead of their words, I listen to the
    music of the women's voices.

Some family business must be being resolved: Renée is agitated,
    her tone suddenly urgent,
there's something she's been waiting to tell; her eyes hold on
    Catherine's and it's that,
the intensity of her gaze, that brings back to me how Catherine
    looked during her labor—
all those hours—then, the image startlingly vivid, I see Renée giv-
    ing birth to Catherine.

I see the darkened room, then the bed, then, sinews drawn tight
    in her neck, Renée herself,
with the same abstracted look in her eyes that Catherine had, layer
    on layer of self disadhering,
all the dross gone, all but the fire of concentration, the heart-stop-
    ping beauty, and now,
at last, my Catherine, our Catherine, here for us all, blazing, bawl-
    ing, lacquered with gore.

❖ TIME: 1976

1.

Time for my break; I'm walking from my study down the long
    hallway towards the living room.
Catherine is there, on the couch, reading to Jed, the phonograph
    is playing Bach's *Offering*.
I can just hear Catherine's voice as she shows Jed the pictures:
    Voilà le château, voilà Babar,
and with no warning I'm taken with a feeling that against all logic
    I recognize to be regret,
as violent and rending a regret as anything I've ever felt, and I
    understand immediately
that all of this familiar beating and blurring, the quickening breath,
    the gathering despair,
almost painful all, has to do with the moment I'm in, and my mind,
    racing to keep order,
thrusts this way and that and finally casts itself, my breath along
    with it into the future.

2.

Ten years from now, or twenty; I'm walking down the same hall-
    way, I hear the same music,
the same sounds—Catherine's story, Jed's chirps of response—
    but I know with anxiety
that most of this is only in my mind: the reality is that Catherine
    and Jed are no longer there,

(117)

that I'm merely constructing this—what actually accompanies me
    down that corridor is memory:
here, in this tentative but terribly convincing future I think to
    myself that it must be the music—
the Bach surely is real, I can *hear* it—that drives me so poignantly,
    expectantly back
to remember again that morning of innocent peace a lifetime ago
    when I came towards them;
the sunny room, the music, the voices, each more distinct now:
    Voilà le château, voilà Babar . . .

3.

But if I'm torn so with remembrance in *this* present, then some-
    thing here must be lost.
Has Jed grown, already left home? Has Catherine gone on some-
    where, too, to some other life?
But no, who'd have played the record: perhaps they, or one of them,
    either one would be enough,
will still be out there before me, not speaking, perhaps reading,
    looking out the window, waiting.
Maybe all this grief, then, was illusion; a sadness, not for loss, but
    for the nature of time:
in my already fading future, I try to find a reconciliation for one
    more imaginary absence . . .
All this, sensation, anxiety, and speculation, goes through me in
    an instant, then in another,
a helplessness at what mind will do, then back into the world:
    Voilà Babar, voilà la vieille dame . . .

❖ BIOPSY

Have I told you, love, about the experience
I used to have before I knew you?
At first it seemed a dream—I'd be in bed—
then I'd realize I was awake, which made it—
it was already frightening—appalling.

A dense, percussive, pulsing hum,
too loud to bear as soon as I'd hear it,
it would become a coil of audible matter
tightening over me, so piercing
I was sure I'd tear apart in it.

I'd try to say a word to contradict it,
but its hold on me was absolute,
I was paralyzed; then, my terror
past some limit, I'd try again: this time
I'd cry out aloud, and it would stop.

Trembling, I'd come to myself, as,
the night of your tests, I came shuddering
awake, my fear for you, for both of us,
raging more terribly through me
than that vision of annihilation ever did.

It was like the desolate time before you:
I couldn't turn to you for reassurance
lest I frighten you, couldn't embrace you

for fear I'd wake you to your own anxiety,
so, as I had then, I lay helpless, mute.

The results were "negative"; now
I'll tell you of those hours in which my life,
not touching you but holding you,
not making a sound but crying for you,
divided back into the half it is without you.

❖ TIME: 1978

1.

What could be more endearing, on a long, too quiet, lonely evening
    in an unfamiliar house,
than, on the table before us, Jed's sneakers, which, finally, at eleven
    o'clock, I notice,
tipped on their sides, still tied, the soles barely scuffed since we
    just bought them today,
or rather submitted to Jed's picking them out, to his absolutely
    having to have them,
the least practical pair, but the first thing besides toys he's ever
    cared so much about,
and which, despite their impossible laces and horrible color, he
    passionately wanted, *desired,*
and coerced us into buying, by, when we made him try on the
    sensible pair we'd chosen,
limping in them, face twisted in torment: his first anguished or-
    deal of a violated aesthetic.

2.

What more endearing except Jed himself, who, now, perhaps be-
    cause of the new night noises,
wakes, and, not saying a word, pads in to sit on Catherine's lap,
    head on her breast, silent,
only his breathing, sleep-quickened, as I write this, trying to get it
    all in, hold the moments

between the sad isolation I thought if not to avert then to dimin-
    ish in writing it down,
and this, now, my pen scratching, eyes rushing to follow the line
    and not lose Jed's gaze,
which dims with sleep now, wanders to the window—hills, brush,
    field cleft with trenches—
and begins to flutter so that I can't keep up with it: quick, quick,
    before you're asleep,
listen, how and whenever if not now, now, will I speak to you,
    both of you, of all this?

❖ SOME OF THE FORMS OF JEALOUSY

Signs

My friend's wife has a lover; I come to this conclusion—not sus-
  picion, mind, conclusion,
not a doubt about it, not a hesitation, although how I get there
  might be hard to track;
a blink a little out of phase, say, with its sentence, perhaps a word
  or two too few;
a certain tenderness of atmosphere, of aura, almost like a preg-
  nancy, with less glow, perhaps,
but similar complex inward blushes of accomplishment, achieve-
  ment, pride—during dinner,
as she passes me a dish of something, as I fork a morsel of it off, as
  our glances touch.

My friend's manner, or his guise, is openness, heartiness and
  healthy haleness in all things;
the virtue of conviction, present moment, that sort of thing: it is
  his passion and his ethic,
so I don't know now if he knows or doesn't know, or knows and
  might be hiding it, or doesn't care.
He is hearty, open, present; he is eating dinner in the moment
  with his wife and old dear friend.
The wife, wifely, as she pours my wine and hands it to me looks
  across the glass's rim at me.
Something in the wifely glance tells me now she knows I know,
  and when I shyly look away,

reach across for bread and butter, she looks down at my hand, and
up again: she is telling me
she doesn't care the least bit if I know or don't know, she might in
fact wish me to know.

My friend is in the present still, taking sustenance; it's sustaining,
good; he smiles, good.
Down below, I can just make out the engines of his ship, the
stresses, creaks, and groans;
everything's in hand; I hear the happy workers at their chugging
furnaces and boilers.
I let my friend's guise now be not my guise but truth; in truth, I'm
like him, dense, convinced,
involved all in the moment, hearty, filled, fulfilled, not just with
manner, but with fact.
I ply my boilers, too; my workers hum: light the deck lamps, let
the string quartet play.

My friend's wife smiles and offers me her profile now; she is tell-
ing me again: but why?
She smiles again, she glows, she plays me like a wind chime; I sit
here clanging to myself.
My friend doesn't seem to see me resonating; he grins, I grin, too,
I flee to him again.
I'm with him in his moment now, I'm in my mouth just as he's in
his, munching, hungrily, heartily.
My safe and sane and hungry mouth hefts the morsels of my sus-
tenance across its firmament.
The wife smiles yet again, I smile, too, but what I'm saying is if
what she means is so,

I have no wish to know; more, I never did know; more, if by any
  chance I might have known,
I've forgotten, absolutely, yes: if it ever did come into my mind it's
  slipped my mind.
In truth, I don't remember anything; I eat, I drink, I smile; I hardly
  even know I'm there.

Baby Talk

Willa Selenfriend likes Paul Peterzell better than she likes me
  and I am dying of it.
"Like" is what we say in eighth grade to mean a person has a secret
  crush on someone else.
I am dying of Willa liking Paul without knowing why she likes
  him more, or what it means.
It doesn't matter, Willa has insinuated cells of doubt in me, I al-
  ready feel them multiplying,
I know already that a single lifetime won't be long enough to extir-
  pate their progeny.
Willa likes Paul better than me but one summer day she'll come
  out to the park with me.
Why? Did she pity me? I don't care. We're there, we've walked,
  now we're resting on the grass.
Is this rest, though, to lie here, Willa so close, as lovely as ever, and
  as self-possessed?
I try, too, to calm myself, but the silence is painful; is this because
  Paul's in it, too?
Do I suspect it's that of which Willa's silence is composed? If so,
  of what is mine composed?
We lie there just a minute, or a year, the surgings and the pulsings
  in my heart and groin

(125)

are so intense that finally Paul's forgotten, only Willa's there with
    me, my docile longings.
Willa's turned towards me, her eyes are closed, I bring my face
    down closer, next to hers.
Astonishing that Willa should be in the visible with me, glowing
    in the world of pertinent form.
I move my lips towards hers, I can't resist, only this much, this
    gently, but then, no,
with one subtle shift, the mildest movement of the angle of her
    brow, Willa repositions us
so that my awkwardness makes absurd my plot of our participa-
    tion in a mutual sensual accord.
With what humiliating force I have to understand I'd been suf-
    fering an unforgivable illusion;
I'd believed that for a little moment Paul had left us, but he'd been
    there all along,
with the unwavering omniscience of a parent, the power of what
    someday I'll call a conscience.
What had ever made me think I'd so easily obliterate him from
    the fraying dusk of childhood?
Weren't we contained in him, held in him; wouldn't fearful heart
    forever now falter in its flight?

The Cautionary

A man who's married an attractive, somewhat younger woman
    conceives a painful jealousy of her.
At first he's puzzled as to why he should brood so fretfully on her
    faithfulness or lack of it.
Their lovemaking is fulfilling: he enjoys it, his wife seems to, too,
    as much as he does,

or, to his surprise (he's never had this experience before), maybe
     more than he does.
When they married, it had seemed a miracle, he'd hardly been
     able to believe his great luck:
the ease and grace with which she'd come to him, the frank, good-
     humored way she'd touch him.
But now . . . it isn't that she gives too much meaning to sex, or
     exhibits insufficient affection,
it's how *involved* in it she gets, so nearly oblivious, in a way he can
     never imagine being.
He finds that he's begun to observe their life in bed with what he
     thinks is a degree of detachment.
He sees himself, his blemishes, the paunch he can't always hide,
     then her, her sheen, her glow.
Why, he asks, would such a desirable woman have committed
     herself so entirely to such as him?
And, more to the point: why this much passion, these urgencies
     and wants, this blind delight?
By a train of logic he can't trace to its source but which he finds
     chillingly irrefutable,
he decides that it's not he himself, as himself, his wife desires, but
     that she simply *desires*.
He comes to think he's incidental to this desire, which is general,
     unspecific, without object,
almost, in its intensity and heat, without a subject: she herself
     seems secondary to it,
as though the real project of her throaty, heaving passion was to
     melt her mindlessly away.
Why would such need be limited to him: wouldn't it sweep like a
     searchlight across all maleness?

He can't help himself, he begins to put to the proof his disturbing
 but compelling observations.
When they're out together, it's self-evident to him that every man
 who sees her wants her:
all the furtive glances, behind, aside, even into surfaces that hold
 her image as she passes.
It dawns on him in a shocking and oddly exciting insight that for
 so many to desire her
some *signal* would have to be sent, not an actual gesture perhaps,
 nothing so coarse as a beckoning,
but something like an aura, of eagerness, availability, which she'd
 be subconsciously emitting.
Hardly noticing, he falls a step behind her, the better to watch
 her, to keep track of her.
Then he realizes to his chagrin that his scrutiny might very well
 be working on his wife.
In a sadly, self-fulfilling prophecy, she might begin to feel vulnera-
 ble, irritated, disconnected;
yes, alone, she must often feel alone, as though he, wretch that he
 is, wasn't even there.
This is the last way he'd have thought that his obsession would
 undo him, but why not?
A woman among admiring men is already in the broadest sense a
 potential object of desire,
but a woman with a sharply heightened awareness of her most
 elementary sexual identity,
as his wife by now would have, with this jackal, as he now sees
 himself, sniffing behind her:
wouldn't she, even against her best intentions, manifest this in a
 primitive, perceptible way,

and wouldn't men have to be aware, however vaguely, that some
sexual event was taking place?
Mightn't the glances she'd inspire reflect this, bringing an intrigu-
ing new sense of herself,
and mightn't this make even more likely that she'd betray him in
just the way that he suspects?
Yes. No. Yes. He knows that he should stop all this: but how can
he, without going to the end?
The end might be just the thing he's driving them both towards,
he can't help himself, though,
he'll dissemble his fixations, but if there's to be relief, it will have
to wait till then.

Politics

They're discussing the political situation they've been watching
evolve in a faraway country.
He's debating intensely, almost lecturing, about fanaticism and
religion, the betrayal of ideals.
He believes he's right, but even as he speaks he knows within him-
self that it's all incidental;
he doesn't really care that much, he just can't help himself, what
he's really talking about
is the attraction that he feels she feels towards those dark and
passionate young men
just now glowing on the screen with all the unimpeachable right-
eousness of the once-oppressed.
He says that just because they've been afflicted isn't proof against
their lying and conniving.
What he means is that they're not, because she might find them
virile, therefore virtuous.

(129)

He says that there are always forces we don't see that use these
things for evil ends.
What he means is that he's afraid that she might turn from him
towards someone suffering,
or, as possible, towards someone who'd share with similar convic-
tion her abhorrence of suffering.
He means he's troubled by how *sure* she is, how her compassions
are so woven into her identity.
Isn't the degree to which she's certain of her politics, hence of her
rightness in the world,
the same degree to which she'd be potentially willing to risk her-
self, and him, and everything?
Also, should she wish to justify an action in her so firmly grounded
socio-ethical system,
any action, concupiscence, promiscuity, orgy, wouldn't it not only
let her but abet her?
Sometimes he feels her dialectics and her assurance are assertions
of some ultimate availability.
Does he really want someone so self-sufficient, who knows her-
self so well, knows so much?
In some ways, he thinks—has he really come to this?—he might
want her knowing *nothing*.
No, not nothing, just ... a little less ... and with less fervor, greater
pragmatism, realism.
More and more in love with her, touched by her, he still goes on,
to his amazement, arguing.

The Question

The middle of the night, she's wide awake, carefully lying as far
    away as she can from him.

He turns in his sleep and she can sense him realizing she's not in
    the place she usually is,

then his sleep begins to change, he pulls himself closer, his arm
    comes comfortably around her.

"Are you awake?" she says, then, afraid that he might think she's
    asking him for sex,

she hurries on, "I want to know something; last summer, in Cleve-
    land, did you have someone else?"

She'd almost said—she was going to say—"Did you have a *lover?*"
    but she'd caught herself;

she'd been frightened by the word, she realized; it was much too
    definite, at least for now.

Even so, it's only after pausing that he answers, "No," with what
    feeling she can't tell.

He moves his hand on her, then with a smile in his voice asks,
    "Did you have somebody in Cleveland?"

"That's not what I was asking you," she says crossly. "But that's
    what I asked *you,*" he answers.

She's supposed to be content now, the old story, she knows that
    she's supposed to be relieved,

but she's not relieved, her tension hasn't eased the slightest bit,
    which doesn't surprise her.

She's so confused that she can't really even say now if she wants to
    believe him or not.

Anyway, what about that pause? Was it because in the middle of
    the night and six months later

he wouldn't have even known what she was talking about, or was
      it because he needed that moment
to frame an answer which would neutralize what might after all
      have been a shocking thrust
with a reasonable deflection, in this case, his humor: a laugh that's
      like a lie and is.
"When would I have found the time" he might have said, or, "Who
      in Cleveland could I love?"
Or, in that so brief instant, might he have been finding a way to
      stay in the realm of the truth,
as she knew he'd surely want to, given how self-righteously he es-
      teemed his ethical integrities?
It comes to her with a start that what she most deeply and pain-
      fully suspects him of is a *renunciation*.
She knows that he has no one now; she thinks she knows there's
      been no contact from Cleveland,
but she still believes that there'd been something then, and if it
      was as important as she thinks,
it wouldn't be so easily forgotten, it would still be with him some-
      where as a sad regret,
perhaps a precious memory, but with that word, renunciation,
      hooked to it like a price tag.
Maybe that was what so rankled her, that she might have been the
      object of his charity, his *goodness*.
That would be too much; that he would have wronged her, then
      sacrificed himself for her.
Yes, "Lover," she should have said it, "Lover, lover," should have made
      him try to disavow it.
She listens to his breathing: he's asleep again, or has he taught
      himself to feign that, too?

"No, last summer in Cleveland I didn't have a lover, I have never
      been to Cleveland, I love you.
There is no Cleveland, I adore you, and, as you'll remember, there
      was no last summer:
the world last summer didn't yet exist, last summer still was uni-
      versal darkness, chaos, pain."

The Mirror

The way these days she dresses with more attention to go out to
      pass the afternoon alone,
shopping or just taking walks, she says, than when they go to-
      gether to a restaurant or party:
it's such a subtle thing, how even speak of it, how imagine he'd be
      able to explain it to her?
The way she looks for such long moments in the mirror as she
      gets ready, putting on her makeup;
the way she looks so deeply at herself, gazes at her eyes, her mouth,
      down along her breasts:
what is he to say, that she's looking at herself in ways he's never
      seen before, more *carnally?*
She would tell him he was mad, or say something else he doesn't
      want no matter what to hear.
The way she puts her jacket on with a flourish, the way she gaily
      smiles going out the door,
the door, the way the door slams shut, the way its latch clicks shut
      behind her so emphatically.
What is he to think? What is he to say, to whom? The mirror,
      jacket, latch, the awful door?

He can't touch the door, he's afraid he'll break the frightening cov-
enant he's made with it.
He can't look into the mirror, either, that dark, malicious void:
who knows what he might see?

The Silence

He hasn't taken his eyes off you since we walked in, although you
seem not to notice particularly.
Only sometimes, when your gaze crosses his, mightn't it leave a
very tiny *tuft* behind?
It's my imagination surely, but mightn't you be all but imper-
ceptibly acknowledging his admiration?
We've all known these things; the other, whom we've never seen
before, but whose ways we recognize,
and with whom we enter into brilliant complicities; soul's recep-
tors tuned and armed;
the concealed messages, the plots, the tactics so elegant they might
have been rehearsed:
the way we wholly disregard each other, never, except at the most
casually random intervals,
let our scrutinies engage, but then that deep, delicious draft, that
eager passionate appreciation . . .
I tell myself that I don't care, as I might not sometimes, when no
rival's happened by,
but I do care now, I care acutely, I just wonder what the good
would be if I told you I can see
your mild glances palpably, if still so subtly, furtively, intertwining
now with his?
I'd only be insulting you, violating my supposed trust in you, be-
littling both of us.

(134)

We've spent so much effort all these years learning to care for one
    another's sensitivities.
In an instant that's all threatened; your affections seem as tenuous
    as when we met,
and I have to ask myself, are you more valuable to me the more
    that you're at risk?
Am I to you? It's degrading, thinking we're more firmly held to-
    gether by our mutual anxiety.
If my desire is susceptible to someone else's valuations of its ob-
    ject, then what am I?
Can I say that my emotions are my own if in my most intimate
    affection such contaminations lurk?
Still, though, what if this time I'd guessed right, and what if I
    should try to tell you,
to try to laugh about it with you, to use our union, and our hard-
    earned etiquettes to mock him,
this intruder—look—who with his dream of even daring to at-
    tempt you would be ludicrous?
There would still be risks I almost can't let myself consider: that
    you'd be humoring me,
that the fierce intensity of your attraction to him would already
    constitute a union with him,
I'd be asking you to lie and doing so you'd be thrown more em-
    phatically into his conspiracy;
your conniving with him would relegate me to the status of an
    obligation, a teary inconvenience.
This is so exhausting: when will it relent? It seems never, not as
    long as consciousness exists.
Therefore, as all along I knew I would, as I knew I'd have to, I
    keep still, conceal my sorrow.
Therefore, when you ask, "Is something wrong?" what is there to
    answer but, "Of course not, why?"

Soliloquies

1.

Strange that sexual jealousy should be so much like sex itself: the
      same engrossing reveries,
the intricate, voluptuous pre-imaginings, the impatient plottings
      towards a climax, then climax . . .
Or, not quite climax, since jealousy is different in how uninvolved
      it is in consummation.
What is its consummation but negation? Not climax but relief, a
      sigh of resignation, disappointment.
Still, how both depend upon a judicious intermingling of the imagi-
      nary and the merely real,
and how important image is for both, the vivid, breath-held un-
      scrolling of fugitive inner effigies.
Next to all our other minds, how pure both are, what avid con-
      centration takes us in them.
Maybe this is where jealousy's terrific agitation comes from, be-
      cause, in its scalding focus,
a desperate single-mindedness is imposed upon the soul and the
      sad, conditioned soul responds,
so fervently, in such good faith, it hardly needs the other person
      for its delicious fever.
Is there anything in life in which what is fancied is so much more
      intense than what's accomplished?
We know it's shadow, but licentious consciousness goes on for-
      ever manufacturing . . . fever.

2.

The stupidity of it, the repetitiveness, the sense of all one's mental
mechanisms run amok.

Knowing that pragmatically, statistically, one's fantasies are fool-
ish, but still being trapped.

The almost unmanageable foreboding that one's character won't
be up to its own exigencies.

Knowing one is one's own victim; how self-diminishing to have to
ask, "Who really *am* I, then?"

I am someone to be rescued from my mind, but the agent of my
suffering is its sole redemption;

only someone else, a specific someone else, can stop me from in-
flicting this upon myself.

And so within myself, in this unsavory, unsilent solitude of self, I
fall into an odious dependency.

I'm like an invalid relying absolutely on another's rectitude; but
the desperate invalid, abandoned,

would have at least the moral compensation of knowing that he
wasn't doing this to himself;

philosophically, his reliance would be limited by the other's sense
of obligation, or its absence.

This excruciating, groundless need becomes more urgent, more to
be desired the more it's threatened,

while its denouement promises what one still believes will be an
unimaginably luxurious release.

3.

I try to imagine the kind of feeling which would come upon me if
I really were betrayed now.

How long would I remain in that abject state of mind? When
would it end? Am I sure it would?

What constitutes a state of mind at all? Certain chunks of feeling,
of pleasure or pain?

I postulate the pain, but can I really? My mood prevents it. Is that
all I am, then, mood?

Sometimes I feel firmly socketed within myself; other moments, I
seem barely present.

Which should I desire? Mightn't it be better not to feel anything
if I'm helpless anyway?

I try to reconceive the problem: I am he who will forgive his being
wronged, but can I know I will?

All my mind will tell me absolutely and obsessively is that its fu-
ture isn't in my governance.

Might that be why the other's possible offense seems much more
rank than mine would ever be?

My betrayal would be whimsical, benign, the hymen of my inno-
cence would be quickly reaffirmed.

Hers infects, contaminates, is ever the first premeditated step of
some squalid longer term.

I would forgive, but suspect that she might already be beyond for-
giveness: whose fault then?

4.

What would be the difference? The way jealousy seeps into my
    notions of intention and volition,
the annihilating force it has: mightn't it be grounded in the furies
    of more radical uncertainty?
That nothing lasts, that there's no real reason why it doesn't last,
    and that there's death,
and more maddening still that existence has conjectured possi-
    bilities of an after-death,
but not their certainty, rather more the evidence that any endless-
    ness is mental fiction.
And that there might be a God, a potentially beloved other who
    would know, this, and everything,
who already has sufficient knowledge of our fate to heal us but
    may well decide not to do so.
How not rage, how, in love, with its promises of permanence, the
    only answer to these doubts,
not find absurd that this, too, should suffer from foreboding, and
    one so mechanically averted?
Might jealousy finally suggest that what we're living isn't ever what
    we think we are?
What, though, would more require our love, our being loved, our
    vow of faithfulness and faith?
And what would more compel that apprehensive affirmation: *I'll
    love you forever, will you me?*

❖ REALMS

Often I have thought that after my death, not in death's void as we
usually think it,
but in some simpler after-realm of the mind, it will be given to me
to transport myself
through all space and all history, to behold whatever and converse
with whomever I wish.

Sometimes I might be an actual presence, a traveller listening at
the edge of the crowd;
at other times I'd have no physical being; I'd move unseen but
seeing through palace or slum.
Sophocles, Shakespeare, Bach! Grandfathers! Homo-erectus! The
universe bursting into being !

Now, though, as I wake, caught by some imprecise longing, you in
the darkness beside me,
your warmth flowing gently against me, it comes to me that in all
my after-death doings,
I see myself as alone, always alone, and I'm suddenly stranded,
forsaken, desperate, lost.

To propel myself through those limitless reaches without you!
Never! Be with me, come!
Babylon, Egypt, Lascaux, the new seas boiling up life; Dante,
Delphi, Magyars and Mayans!
Wait, though, it must be actually you, not my imagination of you,
however real: for myself,

mind would suffice, no matter if all were one of time's terrible
      toys, but I must have you,
as you are, the unquenchable fire of your presence, otherwise death
      truly would triumph.
Quickly, never mind death, never mind mute, oblivious, onrush-
      ing time: wake, hold me!

❖ LOST WAX

My love gives me some wax,
so for once instead of words
I work at something real;
I knead until I see emerge
a person, a protagonist;
but I must overwork my wax,
it loses its resiliency,
comes apart in crumbs.

I take another block:
this work, I think, will be a self;
I can feel it forming, brow
and brain; perhaps it will be me,
perhaps, if I can create myself,
I'll be able to mend myself;
my wax, though, freezes
this time, fissures, splits.

Words or wax, no end
to our self-shaping, our forlorn
awareness at the end of which
is only more awareness.
Was ever truth so malleable?
Arid, inadhesive bits of matter.
What might heal you? Love.
What make you whole? Love. My love.

❖ GRACE

Almost as good as her passion, I'll think, almost as good as her
     presence, her physical grace,
almost as good as making love with her, I'll think in my last ach-
     ing breath before last,
my glimpse before last of the light, were her good will and good
     wit, the steadiness of her affections.

Almost, I'll think, sliding away on my sleigh of departure, the rind
     of my consciousness thinning,
the fear of losing myself, of—worse—losing her, subsiding as I
     think, hope it must,
almost as good as her beauty, her glow, was the music of her
     thought, her voice and laughter.

Almost as good as kissing her, being kissed back, I hope I'll have
     strength still to think,
was watching her as she worked or read, was beholding her self-
     less sympathy for son, friend, sister,
even was feeling her anger, sometimes, rarely, lift against me, then
     be forgotten, put aside.

Almost, I'll think, as good as our unlikely coming together, was
     our constant, mostly unspoken debate
as to whether good in the world was good in itself, or (my side)
     only the absence of evil:
no need to say how much how we lived was shaped by her bright
     spirit, her humor and hope.

Almost as good as living at all—improbable gift—was watching
    her once cross our room,
the reflections of night rain she'd risen to close the window against
    flaring across her,
doubling her light, then feeling her come back to bed, reaching to
    find and embrace me,

as I'll hope she'll be there to embrace me as I sail away on the last
    voyage out of myself,
that last, sorrowful passage out of her presence, though her pres-
    ence, I'll think, will endure,
as firmly as ever, as good even now, I'll think in that lull before
    last, almost as ever.

❖ HELEN

1.

More voice was in her cough tonight: its first harsh, stripping sound
   would weaken abruptly,
and he'd hear the voice again, not hers, unrecognizable, its notes
   from somewhere else,
someone saying something they didn't seem to want to say, in a
   tongue they hadn't mastered,
or a singer, diffident and hesitating, searching for a place to start
   an unfamiliar melody.

Its pitch was gentle, almost an interrogation, intimate, a plea, a
   moan, almost sexual,
but he could hear assertion, too, a straining from beneath, a forc-
   ing at the withheld consonant,
and he realized that she was holding back, trying with great effort
   not to cough again,
to change the spasm to a tone instead and so avert the pain that
   lurked out at the stress.

Then he heard her lose her almost-word, almost-song: it became
   a groan, the groan a gasp,
the gasp a sigh of desperation, then the cough rasped everything
   away, everything was cough now,
he could hear her shuddering, the voice that for a moment seemed
   the gentlest part of her,
choked down, effaced, abraded, taken back, as all of her was being
   taken from him now.

2.

In the morning she was standing at the window, he lay where he
      was and quietly watched her.
A sound echoed in from somewhere, she turned to listen, and he
      was shocked at how she moved;
not *enough* moved, just her head, pivoting methodically, the mech-
      anisms slowed nearly to a halt,
as though she was afraid to jar herself with the contracting ten-
      dons and skeletal leverings.

A flat, cool, dawn light washed in on her: how pale her skin was,
      how dull her tangled hair.
So much of her had burned away, and what was left seemed draped
      listlessly upon her frame.
It was her eye that shocked him most, though; he could only see
      her profile, and the eye in it,
without fire or luster, was strangely isolated from her face, and
      even from her character.

For the time he looked at her, the eye existed not as her eye, his
      wife's, his beloved's eye,
but as *an* eye, an object, so emphatic, so pronounced, it was separ-
      ate both from what it saw
and from who saw with it: it could have been a creature's eye, a
      member of that larger class
which simply indicated sight and not that essence which her glance
      had always brought him.

It came to him that though she hadn't given any sign, she knew
    that he was watching her.
He was saddened that she'd tolerate his seeing her as she was now,
    weak, disheveled, haggard.
He felt that they were both involved, him watching, her letting
    him, in a depressing indiscretion:
she'd always, after all their time together, only offered him the
    images she thought he wanted.

She'd known how much he needed beauty, how much presumed
    it as the elemental of desire.
The loveliness that illuminated her had been an engrossing nar-
    rative his spirit fed on;
he entered it and flowed out again renewed for having touched
    within and been a part of it.
In his meditations on her, he'd become more complicated, fuller,
    more essential to himself.

It was to her beauty he'd made love at first, she was there within
    its captivating light,
but was almost secondary, as though she was just the instance of
    some overwhelming generality.
She herself was shy before it; she, too, as unassumingly as possible
    was testing this abstraction
which had taken both of them into its sphere, rendering both
    subservient to its serene enormity.

As their experience grew franker, and as she learned to move more
    confidently towards her core,
became more overly active in elaborating needs and urges, her
    beauty still came first.

(147)

In his memory, it seemed to him that they'd unsheathed her from
the hazes of their awe,
as though her unfamiliar, fiery, famished nakedness had been dis-
closed as much to her as him.

She'd been grateful to him, and that gratitude became in turn an-
other fact of his desire.
Her beauty had acknowledged him, allowed him in its secret pre-
cincts, let him be its celebrant,
an implement of its luxurious materiality, and though he remained
astonished by it always,
he fulfilled the tasks it demanded of him, his devotions rein-
vigorated and renewed.

3.

In the deepest sense, though, he'd never understood what her
beauty was or really meant.
If you only casually beheld her, there were no fanfares, you were
taken by no immolating ecstasies.
It amused him sometimes seeing other men at first not really un-
derstand what they saw;
no one dared to say it, but he could feel them holding back their
disappointment or disbelief.

Was this Helen, mythic Helen, this female, fleshed like any other,
imperfect and approachable?
He could understand: he himself, when he'd first seen her, hadn't
really; he'd even thought,
before he'd registered her spirit and intelligence, before her laugh-
ter's melodies had startled him—

if only one could alter such and such, improve on this or that: he
hardly could believe it now.

But so often he'd watched others hear her speak, or laugh, look at
her again, and fall in love,
as puzzled as he'd been at the time they'd wasted while their rap-
tures of enchantment took.
Those who hadn't ever known her sometimes spoke of her as
though she were his thing, his toy,
but that implied something static in her beauty, and she was surely
just the opposite of that.

If there was little he'd been able to explain of what so wonderfully
absorbed him in her,
he knew it was a movement and a process, that he was taken to-
wards and through her beauty,
touched by it but even more participating in its multiplicities, the
revelations of its grace.
He felt himself becoming real in her, tangible, as though before
he'd only half existed.

Sometimes he would even feel it wasn't really him being brought
to such unlikely fruition.
Absurd that anyone so coarse and ordinary should be in touch
with such essential mystery:
something else, beyond him, something he would never under-
stand, used him for its affirmations.
What his reflections came to was something like humility, then a
gratitude of his own.

4.

The next night her cough was worse, with a harsher texture, the
    spasms came more rapidly,
and they'd end with a deep, complicated emptying, like the whin-
    ing flattening of a bagpipe.
The whole event seemed to need more labor: each cough sounded
    more futile than the last,
as though the effort she'd made and the time lost making it had
    added to the burden of illness.

Should he go to her? He felt she'd moved away from him, turning
    more intently towards herself.
Her sickness absorbed her like a childbirth; she seemed almost
    like someone he didn't know.
There'd been so many Helens, the first timid girl, then the sen-
    sual Helen of their years together,
then the last, whose grace had been more intricate and difficult to
    know and to exult in.

How childishly frightened he'd always been by beauty's absence,
    by its destruction or perversity.
For so long he let himself be tormented by what he knew would
    have to happen to her.
He'd seen the old women as their thighs and buttocks bloated,
    then withered and went slack,
as their dugs dried, skin dried, legs were sausaged with the veins
    that rose like kelp.

He'd tried to overcome himself, to feel compassion towards them,
but, perhaps because of her,
he'd felt only a shameful irritation, as though they were colluding
in their loss.
Whether they accepted what befell them, even, he would think,
gladly acquiescing to it,
or fought it, with all their sad and valiant unguents, dyes, and oint-
ments, was equally degrading.

His own body had long ago become a ruin, but beauty had never
been a part of what he was.
What would happen to his lust, and to his love, when time came
to savage and despoil her?
He already felt his will deserting him; for a long time, though,
nothing touched or dulled her;
perhaps she really was immortal, maybe his devotion kept her from
the steely rakings of duration.

Then, one day, something at her jowls; one day her lips; one day
the flesh at her elbows . . .
One day, one day, one day he looked at her and knew that what
he'd feared so was upon them.
He couldn't understand how all his worst imaginings had come to
pass without his noticing.
Had he all this while been blind, or had he not wanted to ac-
knowledge what he'd dreaded?

He'd been gazing at her then; in her wise way, she'd looked back at
him and touched him,
and he knew she'd long known what was going on in him; another
admiration took him,

then another fire, and that simply, he felt himself closer to her:
there'd been no trial,
nothing had been lost, of lust, of love, and something he'd never
dreamed would be was gained.

5.

With her in the darkness now, not even touching her, he sensed
her fever's suffocating dryness.
He couldn't, however much he wanted to, not let himself believe
she was to be no more.
And there was nothing he could do for her even if she'd let him; he
tried to calm himself.
Her cough was hollow, soft, almost forgiving, ebbing slowly through
the volumes of her thorax.

He could almost hear that world as though from in her flesh: the
current of her breath,
then her breastbone, ribs, and spine, taking on the cough's vibra-
tions, giving back their own.
Then he knew precisely how she was within herself as well, he
was with her as he'd never been:
he'd unmoored in her, cast himself into the night of her, and per-
ceived her life with her.

All she'd lived through, all she'd been and done, he could feel accu-
mulated in this instant.
The impressions and sensations, feelings, dreams, and memories
were tearing loose in her,
had disconnected from each other and randomly begun to float,
collide, collapse, entangle;

they were boiling in a matrix of sheer chance, suspended in a purely
mental universe of possibility.

He knew that what she was now to herself, what she remembered,
might not in truth have ever been.
Who, then, was she now, who was the person she had been, if all
she was, all he still so adored,
was muddled, addled, mangled: what of her could be repository
now, the place where she existed?
When everything was shorn from her, what within this flux of
fragments still stayed her?

He knew then what he had to do: he was so much of her now and
she of him that she was his,
her consciousness and memory both his, he would will her into
him, keep her from her dissolution.
All the wreckage of her fading life, its shattered hours taken in
this fearful flood,
its moments unrecoverable leaves twirling in a gust across a waste
of loss, he drew into himself,

and held her, kept her, all the person she had been was there within
his sorrow and his longing:
it didn't matter what delirium had captured her, what of her was
being lacerated, rent,
his pain had taken on a power, his need for her became a force
that he could focus on her;
there was something in him like triumph as he shielded her within
the absolute of his affection.

Then he couldn't hold it, couldn't keep it, it was all illusion, a con-
fection of his sorrow:
there wasn't room within the lenses of his mortal being to contain
what she had been,
to do justice to a single actual instant of her life and soul, a single
moment of her mind,
and he released her then, let go of this diminished apparition he'd
created from his fear.

But still, he gave himself to her, without moving moved to her:
she was still his place of peace.
He listened for her breath: was she still here with him, did he have
her that way, too?
He heard only the flow of the silent darkness, but he knew now
that in it they'd become it,
their shells of flesh and form, the old delusion of their separate-
ness and incompletion, gone.

When one last time he tried to bring her image back, she was as
vivid as he'd ever seen her.
What they were together, everything they'd lived, all that seemed
so fragile, bound in time,
had come together in him, in both of them: she had entered death,
he was with her in it.
Death was theirs, she'd become herself again; her final, searing
loveliness had been revealed.

(154)

❖ ARCHETYPES

Often before have our fingers touched in sleep or half-sleep and
    enlaced,
often I've been comforted through a dream by that gently sensi-
    tive pressure,
but this morning, when I woke your hand lay across mine in an
    awkward,
unfamiliar position so that it seemed strangely external to me,
    removed,
an object whose precise weight, volume and form I'd never re-
    marked:
its taut, resistant skin, dense muscle-pads, the subtle, complex
    structure,
with delicately elegant chords of bone aligned like columns in a
    temple.

Your fingers began to move then, in brief, irregular tensions and
    releasings;
it felt like your hand was trying to hold some feathery, fleeting
    creature,
then you suddenly, fiercely, jerked it away, rose to your hands and
    knees,
and stayed there, palms flat on the bed, hair tangled down over
    your face,
until with a coarse sigh almost like a snarl you abruptly let your-
    self fall
and lay still, your hands drawn tightly to your chest, your head
    turned away,

forbidden to me, I thought, by whatever had raised you to that
defiant crouch.

I waited, hoping you'd wake, turn, embrace me, but you stayed in
yourself,
and I felt again how separate we all are from one another, how
even our passions,
which seem to embody unities outside of time, heal only the most
benign divisions,
that for our more abiding, ancient terrors we each have to find our
own valor.
You breathed more softly now, though; I took heart, touched
against you,
and, as though nothing had happened, you opened your eyes,
smiled at me,
and murmured—how almost startling to hear you in your real
voice—"Sleep, love."

❖ OLD MAN

Special: Big Tits, says the advertisement for a soft-core magazine on
   our neighborhood newsstand,
but forget her breasts—a lush, fresh-lipped blonde, skin glowing
   gold, sprawls there, resplendent.
Sixty nearly, yet these hardly tangible, hardly better than harlots
   can still stir me.

Maybe coming of age in the American sensual darkness, never
   seeing an unsmudged nipple,
an uncensored vagina, has left me forever infected with an un-
   quenchable lust of the eye:
always that erotic murmur—I'm hardly myself if I'm not in a state
   of incipient desire.

God knows, though, there are worse twists your obsessions can
   take: last year, in Israel,
a young ultra-Orthodox rabbi, guiding some teen-aged girls
   through the shrine of the *Shoah*,
forbade them to look in one room because there were images in it
   he said were licentious.

The display was a photo: men and women, stripped naked, some
   trying to cover their genitals,
others too frightened to bother, lined up in snow waiting to be
   shot and thrown in a ditch.
The girls to my horror averted their gaze: what carnal mistrust
   had their teacher taught them?

Even that, though . . . Another confession: once, in a book on pre-
   war Poland, a studio-portrait,
an absolute angel, with tormented, tormenting eyes: I kept find-
   ing myself at her page;
that she died in the camps made her, I didn't dare wonder why,
   more present, more precious.

"Died in the camps": that, too, people, or Jews anyway, kept from
   their children back then,
but it was like sex, you didn't have to be told. Sex and death: how
   close they can seem.
So constantly conscious now of death moving towards me, some-
   times I think I confound them.

My wife's loveliness almost consumes me, my passion for her goes
   beyond reasonable bounds;
when we make love, her holding me, everywhere all around me,
   I'm there and not there,
my mind teems, jumbles of faces, voices, impressions: I live my life
   over as though I were drowning.

. . . Then I am drowning, in despair, at having to leave her, this,
   everything, all: unbearable, awful . . .
Still, to be able to die with no special contrition, not having been
   slaughtered or enslaved,
and not having to know history's next mad rage or regression—it
   might be a relief.

No, again no, I don't mean that for a moment, what I mean is the
   world holds me so tightly,

(158)

the good and the bad, my own follies and weakness, that even this
counterfeit Venus,
with her sham heat and her bosom probably plumped with gel, so
moves me my breath catches.

Vamp, siren, seductress, how much more she reveals in her glare
of ink than she knows;
how she incarnates our desperate human need for regard, our pas-
sion to live in beauty,
to be beauty, to be cherished, by glances if by no more, of some-
thing like love, or love.

❖ DROPLETS

Even when the rain falls relatively hard,
only one leaf at a time of the little tree
you planted on the balcony last year,
then another leaf at its time, and one more,
is set trembling by the constant droplets,

but the rain, the clouds flocked over the city,
you at the piano inside, your hesitant music
mingling with the din of the downpour,
the gush of rivulets loosed from the eaves,
the iron railings and flowing gutters,

all of it fuses in me with such intensity
that I can't help wondering why my longing
to live forever has so abated that it hardly
comes to me anymore, and never as it did,
as regret for what I might not live to live,

but rather as a layering of instants like this,
transient as the mist drawn from the rooftops,
yet emphatic as any note of the nocturne
you practice, and, the storm faltering, fading
into its own radiant passing, you practice again.